M

VOLUME FOUR

LOVING

edited by

Deborah Mulhearn

CAPSICA

Mersey Minis

VOLUME FOUR: LOVING

Edited by Deborah Mulhearn
Illustrations by Clare Curtis
Graphic design by Ken Ashcroft
Printed and bound in Italy by Graphicom

ISBN: 978-0-9548431-9-9

First published in September 2007 by Capsica Ltd
83 Ampthill Road, Liverpool L17 9QN, UK

email: merseyminis@capsica.net
www.merseyminis.com
www.loveliverpoolbooks.com

CONTENTS

Dedicated to
Gerry and Beth

INTRODUCTION

LOVING is the fourth volume of Mersey Minis, a series of small books celebrating Liverpool's 800th anniversary.

LOVING is a collection of writing about facets of Liverpool life that have stirred the emotions of visitors and residents alike. The sailor on shore leave, the sentimental tourist, the card-carrying politico and the fervent football fan, LOVING lays bare the often inexplicable passions and partisan feelings that can trigger riots and ructions, and the compulsions that lead people to unexpected places.

A world-renowned scientist discovers how the other half lives when he has to sleep on a park bench. A young actress is thrilled by a ride on the world's first passenger railway and falls for the engineer. There is also an account of a muslim wedding, thought to be the first conducted in England, and the surreal image of the Pope diving into a delirious crowd singing *In My Liverpool Home*.

On the more reflective side, there is the 'expectation exquisitely gratified' for the American who lingered awhile before the pull of London became too great. A consul's wife is bewildered by an English cricket match; foreign industrialists marvel at the new docks; the hearts of refugees are stirred with reminders of home.

The extracts chosen for LOVING reflect the multifarious mix of Lancashire, Irish, Welsh and many other nationalities thrown into the Merseyside melting pot.

LOVING is only a small selection of the immense outpouring of writing that Liverpool has provoked over the years, but the book list directs readers to fuller accounts. The biographies give glimpses into the lives of people who have rekindled some of the significant events in Liverpool's cultural, social and political history and, in the process, revealed something of their own fascinating stories.

DEBORAH MULHEARN

A NOTE ON THE TEXT

The extracts in Mersey Minis are reproduced from original sources, many of which are historic and therefore sometimes using styles and language unfamiliar to modern readers. I have, however, in most cases retained the original spellings, punctuation and sometimes the grammatical mistakes so as not to impede the energy and flow of the writer, and to reflect the uniqueness and idiosyncracy of his or her account.

The date given at the start of each extract is the date the writing refers to, and not necessarily when it was written or published. For publication dates and further details please see the book list on p110.

LOVING

Margaret Simey   1923

Why I fell instantly in love with Liverpool was that in Liverpool I no longer had to lead a double life. The magic of Liverpool is that it is such a conglomerate of people who all insisted on being themselves. There was a Chinese quarter, the Jewish quarter up Brownlow Hill, the Afro Caribbeans down by the river, the Protestants and the Catholics. I felt like a bird released from a cage. I no longer had to pretend that I was in the governing, educated class.

James Johnston Abraham   1911

The sailor is the real king of Liverpool. Everybody in Liverpool loves the sailor, and is only too anxious to show him how to have a good time and spend his money while he is ashore; and it is he is the great man there till he has spent it.

Prince Albert   1846

I cannot get it into my head that there are 250 miles between us! I have done wonders of activity, as you will perhaps have learned from the papers by the time you receive this letter. The loyalty and enthusiasm of the inhabitants are great; but the heat is greater still. I am satisfied that if the population of Liverpool had been weighed this morning, and were to be weighed again now, they would be found many degrees lighter. The docks are wonderful; and the mass of shipping incredible.

George Harrison   1980

Good place to wash your hair, Liverpool. Nice soft water.

Fanny Kemble   1830

We were introduced to the little engine which was to drag us along the rails. She (for they make these curious little fire-horses all mares) consisted of a boiler, a stove, a small platform, a bench, and behind the bench a barrel containing enough water to prevent her being thirsty for fifteen miles, – the whole machine not bigger than a common fire-engine. She goes upon two wheels, which are her feet, and are moved by bright steel legs called pistons; these are propelled by steam, and in proportion as more steam is applied to the upper extremities (the hip-joints, I suppose) of these pistons, the faster they move the wheels; and when it is desirable to diminish the speed, the steam, which unless suffered to

escape would burst the boiler, evaporates through a safety-valve into the air. The reins, bit, and bridle of this wonderful beast is a small steel handle, which applies or withdraws the steam from its legs or pistons, so that a child might manage it. The coals, which are its oats, were under the bench, and there was a small glass tube affixed to the boiler, with water in it, which indicates by its fulness or emptiness when the creature wants water, which is immediately conveyed to it from its reservoirs. There is a chimney to the stove, but as they burn coke there is none of the dreadful black smoke which accompanies the progress of a steam vessel. This snorting little animal, which I felt rather inclined to pat, was then harnessed to our carriage, and, Mr. Stephenson having taken me on the bench of the engine with him, we started at about ten miles an hour. The steam-horse being ill adapted for going up and down hill, the road was kept at a certain level, and appeared sometimes to sink below the surface of the earth, and sometimes to rise above it. Almost at starting it was cut through the solid rock, which formed a wall on either side of it, about sixty feet high. You can't imagine how strange it seemed to be journeying on thus, without any visible cause of progress other than the magical machine, with its flying white breath and rhythmical, unvarying pace, between these rocky walls, which are already clothed with moss and ferns and grasses; and when I reflected that these great masses of stone had been cut asunder to allow our passage thus far below the surface of the earth, I felt as if no fairy tale was ever half so wonderful as what I saw.
******

When I closed my eyes this sensation of flying was quite

delightful, and strange beyond description; yet, strange as it was, I had a perfect sense of security, and not the slightest fear. At one time, to exhibit the power of the engine, having met another steam-carriage which was unsupplied with water, Mr. Stephenson caused it to be fastened in front of ours; moreover, a waggon laden with timber was also chained to us, and thus propelling the idle steam-engine, and dragging the loaded waggon which was beside it, and our own carriage full of people behind, this brave little she-dragon of ours flew on. Farther on she met three carts, which, being fastened in front of her, she pushed on before her without the slightest delay or difficulty; when I add that this pretty little creature can run with equal facility either backward or forward, I believe I have given you an account of all her capacities.

Now for a word or two about the master of all these marvels, with whom I am most horribly in love. He is a man of from fifty to fifty-five years of age; his face is fine, though careworn, and bears an expression of deep thoughtfulness; his mode of explaining his ideas is peculiar and very original, striking, and forcible;  and although his accent indicates strongly his north-country birth, his language has not the slightest touch of vulgarity or coarseness. He has certainly turned my head.

Augustus John ✐   1901

Liverpool, commonly considered a dull, ugly and commercial city, for me abounded in interest and surprise. With what wonderment I explored the sombre district of the Merseyside! This was largely populated by Scandinavian migrants on their way to the New World.

The Goree Piazza, with such a name, for ever reeking of the slave-trade, might still harbour a few superannuated buccaneers musing over their rum: in the Chinese quarter, while visiting certain tenebrous dens, I attempted, but failed, to attain the blissful *Kif* in the company of dishevelled and muttering devotees of the Laughing God: off Scotland Road I penetrated, not without trepidation, into the lodging houses of the Tinkers, where a rough nomadic crew gathered round the communal fire in a spirit of precarious good-fellowship.

Archbishop Derek Worlock   1981

On the feast of Pentecost in 1981 Pope John Paul II celebrated Mass in the Metropolitan Cathedral in Liverpool. Afterwards he went out to the piazza behind the Cathedral, where he was received with great enthusiasm by several thousand young people who were waiting there to greet him. Mostly clad in the red T-shirts of the Youth Service, they cheered, they prayed and they sang hymns and songs for him. Then they linked arms and broke into their favourite anthem, *Bind us together, Lord*, followed with rather greater abandon by *In my Liverpool home.*

The Pope watched and applauded them. Then with great deliberation, as if the play on words had just occurred to him, he went to the microphone and said, 'You are the living

Church of Liverpool.' They cheered loudly and he repeated the phrase several times. Then, unable to resist it any longer, and to the consternation of the special police, present for his security, he dived into their midst, linked arms with some deliriously happy youngsters and joined in to sing *Bind us together in love*.

Charles Dupin   1817

I crossed and re-crossed the Mersey on a steam boat made rather like an Indian double proa. Two identical hulls, long and narrow were arranged parallel but at a certain distance apart. On top was a large platform which carried the steam machinery. The paddle wheel worked in the water between the two hulls. There was a rudder at each end, to save having to change it over in order to go the other way. The smoke from the steam machinery escaped by a chimney which served as the vessel's mast and could, in emergency, carry a square sail. In the middle of the large platform which forms the deck of the boat is a cabin for the passengers, and there is another one for the machinery. Forward, aft and to both sides of the cabins, the platform is sufficiently spacious to transport sheep, cattle, horses and carriages etc.

I took another trip on the Mersey to the mouth of the Duke of Bridgewater's canal. There are three parallel basins, dug alongside each other, but in tiers, and with fine warehouses at their sides, then a flight of locks which climbs the hill. This system of works shows what can be achieved by the wealth, industry and spirit of enterprise of a single individual driven by a noble love of the public good.

George MacDonald Fraser

1909

Inspector Griffin came down to the landing-stage on a raw autumn morning to see the *Mauretania* berthing. It was part of his job; there was always someone from the detective department on hand when the American liners docked, but for Inspector Griffin it was a pleasure, too. He loved the bustle of the wharf at dawn, and the sight of the huge iron ship edging gently into the quay, the busy little tugs, the squealing whistles, the propellor churning the yellow Mersey into dirty foam; he even enjoyed the bite of the wind and the cold drizzle which was causing his colleague, young Constable Murphy, to hunch his collar round his chin as he stamped his feet on the wet flags. To Murphy it was just another tedious chore; he wiped his nose and glowered at the low clouds over the river.

Nik Cohn

1968

Liverpool is a strange town, it gets obsessed by everything it does. It is a seaport and it's made up of different races, it is a city full of neighbourhoods, full of gangs and, outside of Glasgow, it is the rawest, most passionate place in Britain.

 It has a certain black style of its own, a private strength and humour and awareness, real violence, and it is also grim, very much so. After the pubs close down, everyone stands out on corners and watches what happens and has nowhere much

to go. Clubs are small, sweaty and dumb. Kids don't move by themselves or they get nutted by the guerrillas. This is America in England: a night out ends almost inevitably with a punch on the nose.

James Maury 1809

The fourth instant being the anniversary of our independence, the American vessels in this Port displayed their Colours as usual and the crews took holiday to themselves; walking in procession to the Exchange with an American Flag. Whether this gave offence to the British sailors and carpenters or not, I cannot determine, but I expect it did give offence; for a mob rose and either pulled down the American Colours which, in several instances, were torn and destroyed, but by the active interference by the Mayor, quiet was restored in about two hours.

By one side it was alleged that the American sailors treated with indignity a British Jack by hoisting an American one above it. On the other hand our countrymen denied this fact alleging that they were perfectly innocent of the charge.

Both the Mayor and myself have endeavoured to find out the origin of the unpleasant affair, but, as yet, without success.

Be the blame where it may, it is due from me to say the Mayor used every exertion in his power to restore order and to protect our Seamen from the outrage.

Walter Dixon Scott 1907

And with nightfall it emerges as a place of quite exceptional loveliness. That checked curve of the receding buildings, giving the prospect depth without diminution, grades the lights without disparting them, knits them together, both the near and the far, into one exquisitely modulated chorus. Moon-green, mistletoe-white, orange, amethyst, and pearl, are their principal colours, and in this chamber of converging lines the massed clusters branch and leap and linger with the most wonderful effect of tender ardency... Emphatically, a place, this Liverpool, possessing very singular possibilities of beauty.

Nathaniel Hawthorne   1854

June 20th. – The vagabond musicians about town are very numerous. On board the steam ferry-boats, I have heretofore spoken of them. They infest them from May to November, for very little gain apparently. A shilling a day per man must be the utmost of their emolument. It is rather sad to see somewhat respectable old men engaged in this way, with two or three younger associates. Their instruments look much the worse for wear, and even my unmusical ear can distinguish more discord than harmony. They appear to be a very quiet and harmless people. Sometimes there is a woman playing on a fiddle, while her husband blows a wind instrument. In the streets it is not unusual to find a band of half a dozen performers, who, without any provocation or reason whatever, sound their brazen instruments till the houses re-echo. Sometimes one passes a man who stands whistling a tune most unweariably, though I never saw anybody give him anything. The ballad-singers are the strangest, from the total lack of any music in their cracked voices. Sometimes you see a space cleared in the street, and a foreigner playing, while a girl – weather-beaten, tanned, and wholly uncomely in face and shabby in attire – dances ballets. The common people look on, and never criticise or treat any of these poor devils unkindly or uncivilly; but I do not observe that they give them anything.

A crowd – or, at all events, a moderate-sized group – is much more easily drawn together here than with us. The people have a good deal of idle and momentary curiosity, and are always ready to stop when another person has stopped, so as to see what has  attracted his attention. I hardly ever pause to look at a shop-window, without being immediately incommoded by boys and men, who stop likewise, and would forthwith throng the pavement if I did not move on.

Yehudi Menuhin 1932

That beautiful hall in Liverpool, echoing so richly the sounds of the Royal Liverpool Philharmonic has been, ever since I was 13, one of the places I most enjoyed playing in. This association continued through many years, including those memorable years with Sir Charles Groves when we performed a good many works for violin and orchestra together.

Mary Elizabeth Wilson Sherwood 1869

I did not find Liverpool ugly. Her stately public buildings, broad streets, public squares, and noble statues redeem her from the charge; and after a bath, a nap, and an excellent dinner at the comfortable Adelphi we took a drive to a park in the environs, which we found charming. They say the first cathedral you see remains with you forever as the cathedral of the world. Perhaps this first glimpse of an English June and of a European park so favourably impressed me because it was the first, but I am convinced it was charming; so was the fresh-looking, pleasant-spoken English lady whom we met walking in the park, and who so kindly and even learnedly answered our questions about the new trees and flowers.

Jan Molby 1985

Liverpool is full of the kind of people who go out on Monday and couldn't care less about Tuesday morning.

Gorham Parsons Low 1832

The tides in the Mersey rise and fall twenty-five to twenty-eight feet, and consequently the currents are very rapid, and it is only a short time at high water that vessels can go in and go out of the docks. We hauled into King's Dock, it being the only one where tobacco was allowed to be landed, and from there it was put into the King's Warehouse. The duties on it were so enormously high and the temptation to smuggle it so strong, that it was watched day and night with the most jealous care. The Custom House officers had become so shrewd by long practice, that they soon discovered a smuggler, and officers and men were often caught and severely punished. They searched some men almost daily, and if they discovered one cigar or nigger-head of tobacco that they thought was going to be sold or given to a friend, they took it away from the man who had it and sometimes fined him. I have been to Liverpool five voyages and have gone on shore at all times of the day and night, and yet I have never been questioned by a Custom House officer. On that account the sailors used to ask me to take two or three pieces of tobacco ashore for them, but they never persuaded me to do it.

It was about noon when we got our ship into a berth to discharge, and as no fires were allowed within any of the Liverpool docks we had to board on shore. The provisions on board our ship were not nearly so good as they were on the ship on which I had made my first voyage. I have always lived when at sea mostly on bread and coffee. We had now been living for four months on bread that had been on one long voyage and had been baked over again. It was called by sailors 'twice laid bread', and poor at that. The coffee was made of barley and nothing but barley (the only instance I ever knew of its being served to seamen), and the beef was of very inferior quality. The happy change from such food to what we got on shore in the way of roast beef, plum pudding, white bread, and fresh butter, together with milk and real coffee, I remember with satisfaction to this day. But such changes are very trying to the constitution. The men complained that night of feeling a great heaviness. Nevertheless, I have always looked back to that time as an oasis in a sailor's life.

Liverpool is a great commercial city. Vessels of all nations are there. On Sundays, at that time, when they hoisted their colours, the Stars and Stripes showed that the trade with the

United States was greater than with any country. An American hardly felt himself in a foreign country, as there was so much to remind him of home. One day in walking about the town, I was much pleased to find a long street with fine buildings on it called after our Washington. I was always interested in what I saw in connection with farming. When walking around the quays of Liverpool and seeing the immense amount 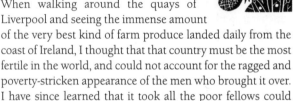 of the very best kind of farm produce landed daily from the coast of Ireland, I thought that that country must be the most fertile in the world, and could not account for the ragged and poverty-stricken appearance of the men who brought it over. I have since learned that it took all the poor fellows could rake and scrape together to pay their rent and taxes.

Hans Gál   1940

31st May Brilliant summer weather. On the road it looks like a seaside resort, only less elegant. An elderly gentleman is walking there, dressed in nothing more than scanty under-pants, which, like all underpants, tend towards an open-door policy. Pot-bellies, hairy chests, South-Sea Island manes, skin colours ranging from lobster red to sepia. Card and chess games are being played in the open air on blankets, sleepers and loungers are lying among the tents, in every available strip of shade. The continuation of Belton Road, beyond the T, forks. To the right it leads to the parade-ground, a large, well-trampled, gravelled square on which the soldiers exercise and where newly-arrived troops of internees have to stand for hours on end with their luggage before they are taken to their quarters. But to the left is a piece of heath-land, uneven and overgrown with grass and nettles. There you stumble over tree-roots, rusty wire and half overgrown ditches, but it is a piece of green, and if you can find a reasonably flat place you can roast there wonderfully in the sun. This meadow is, like all open spaces in our little world, restricted by the barbed wire, and there is an open corner tower with a machine-gun at the ready and a guard who is constantly busy chasing off inquisitive children who approach the barbed wire. We are well and safely guarded! Towards evening, when it gets cooler, Schneider and Sugar, my two friends and room-mates, rush along the less busy path by the parade-ground. They never go otherwise than at the double, and they are engrossed in a serious occupation: they are learning English vocabulary.

Ian Nairn ⌐ 1964

The scale and resilience of the buildings and people is amazing – it is a world city, far more so than London or Manchester. It doesn't feel like anywhere else in Lancashire: comparisons always end up overseas – Dublin, or Boston, or Hamburg.

Charles Dickens ╱ 1867

My Dearest Georgy.
My short report of myself is, that we had an enormous turnaway last night, and do not doubt about having a cram tonight. The day has been very fine, and I have turned it to

the wholesomest account by walking on the sands at New Brighton all the morning. I am not quite right within, but believe it to be an effect of the Railway shaking. There is no doubt of the fact that, after the Staplehurst experience, it tells more and more, instead of (as one might have expected) less and less.

The charming room here, greatly lessens the fatigue of this fatiguing week. I read last night with no more exertion than if I had been at Gad's – and yet to 1100 people, and with astonishing effect. It is Copperfield tonight, and Liverpool is the Copperfield stronghold.

Olaf Stapledon 1913

Next play, by Synge, was roaring comedy, and a skit on Irish peasant life and morals... It is all excitement and jokes and strange Irish oaths and exclamations and weird situations. But the Irish in the gallery could not see Irish morals impugned in this way without hissing and booing and stamping, so that no one heard a word of the last act because of the babel. Not a sound could you hear but angry Irish protest. I don't know why they never got the police in. Liverpool is not used to rowdy theatres I suppose. At Oxford much worse riots were common, but the authorities were always ready with police. Uncle Willie, who was with us, said it was quite a new experience for him. The great joke was that the playboy appeared in a brilliant green and orange striped jersey; and green, you know, is the Nationalist colour, and Orange the Irish Protestant colour. So the colours of the two savage factions that have caused so much rioting in Liverpool were 'sweetly blended in one blinding flash'.

Liverpool Review 1894

There are some people in this world who are foolish enough to hold in light esteem, to speak words of scorning of, and to elevate their noses at, a pastime which has been known to draw together at one assemblage a vast congregation of persons numbering between forty and fifty thousand strong – amply sufficient to people a good-sized town, or to furnish recruits for a fairly formidable army.

None of these superior creatures will be discovered at Goodison Park on Saturday afternoon this week, and none of these people will be missed. A man who can wax sarcastically superior to the hundred and odd thousand sport-lovers who crowd the football enclosures of the United Kingdom every Saturday afternoon is altogether too elevated for common comprehension – he is a chap no fellah can understand.

So we will not apologise to Mr. Minority for having introduced so much football fare into this issue of the *Review*. The end justifies the means, and our end is to entertain as many as possible of the thirty thousand odd footballers who will throng the great Goodison Enclosure on Saturday afternoon. For the hour of the big battle has arrived, and Everton and Liverpool are to meet – at last!

This is a battle for which your football war-horses have been pawing the ground and nostrilling the air for months – nay, years. Several times the clash of arms (and legs) has seemed imminent, but somehow or other public expectation has been repeatedly disappointed, and the clubs have withdrawn their principal weapons of warfare from the field. True, the clubs *have* met ere this, but not in representative fashion. Their second teams have faced each other in combat for the Liverpool Cup, and each of them has a victory recorded to its credit. But now it is unavoidable that the clubs should meet each other representatively, for Liverpool have won their way into the First Division, and Everton are therefore bound to recognise them as foemen worthy of their steel.

Thus has the public palate been whetted for the fray. Even if there were no peculiar history belonging to the clubs, and one was merely the local rival of the other simply because they were both bidders for public favour in the same city, and were therefore bound in duty to struggle each to oust the other and to rise victorious above its neighbour, there would still be a tremendous interest attaching to the first meeting between rivals so prominent in the football world. But as it is there has been a difference between the clubs which smacks of much more than ordinary opposition. The Liverpool Club is in reality a limb of the Everton Club. Their officials were once officials of the Everton Club; their followers were once followers of the Everton Club; and their ground at Anfield was once the Everton ground. A couple of years ago a split took place amongst the working members of the Everton Club, in consequence of differences in regard to the rental of the ground – differences which need not be gone into now, for they have been discussed to death – and the result was that one portion of the members went one way and the other another, the majority of the disputants re-forming the club and acquiring for themselves a new and magnificent centre of operations at Goodison Park, and the minority remaining at the old ground at Anfield, forming themselves into a new club, and commencing to pick up pebbles out of the football brook, *a la* David of old, to cast at the giant Goliath in the camp a little distance away. And now the time has arrived for the slinging of the first pebble, and as David has proved himself well worthy to enter the lists against his formidable enemy, all the city is agog to know whether he will be able to bring down his man.

Edward Lear 1842

I should much like to know – when anyone writes from Knowsley – (for I dare not ask your Lordship – (knowing how much you always have on hand) – for a letter, – though it would please me more than I can express,) to learn if the green plot before the Stillroom window & up to the trees by the Chapel, is yet turned into a Flower

Garden:- and if my unprincipled friend the Chough is still alive & proceeding in his old habits.

Henry James 1869

There is a certain evening that I count as virtually a first impression – the end of a wet, black Sunday, twenty years ago, about the first of March. There had been an earlier vision, but it had turned to grey, like faded ink, and the occasion I speak of was a fresh beginning. No doubt I had mystic prescience of how fond of the murky modern Babylon I was one day to become; certain it is that as I look back I find every small circumstance of those hours of approach and arrival still as vivid as if the solemnity of an opening era had breathed upon it. The sense of approach was already almost tolerably strong at Liverpool, where, as I remember, the perception of the English character of everything was as acute as a surprise, though it could only be a surprise without a shock. It was expectation exquisitely gratified, superabundantly confirmed. There was a kind of wonder, indeed, that England should be as English as, for my entertainment, she took the trouble to be; but the wonder would have been greater, and all the pleasure absent, if the sensation had not been violent. It seems to sit there again like a visiting presence, as it sat opposite to me at breakfast at a small table in a window of the old coffee-room of the Adelphi Hotel – the unextended (as it then was), the unimproved, the unblushingly local Adelphi. Liverpool is not a romantic city, but that smoky Saturday returns to me as a supreme success, measured by its association with the kind of emotion in the hope of which, for the most part, we betake ourselves to far countries.

It assumed this character at an early hour – or rather, indeed, twenty-four hours before – with the sight, as one looked across the wintry ocean, of the strange, dark, lonely freshness of the coast of Ireland. Better still, before we could come up to the city, were the black steamers knocking about in the yellow Mersey, under a sky so low that they seemed to touch it with their funnels, and in the thickest, windiest light. Spring was already in the air, in the town; there was no rain, but there was still less sun – one wondered what had become, on this side of the world, of the big white splotch in the heavens; and the gray mildness, shading away into black at every pretext, appeared in itself a promise. This was how it hung about me, between the window and the fire, in the coffee-room of the hotel – late in the morning for breakfast, as we had been long disembarking. The other passengers had dispersed, knowingly catching trains for London (we had only been a handful); I had the place to myself, and I felt as if I had an exclusive property in the impression. I prolonged it, I sacrificed to it, and it is perfectly recoverable now, with the very taste of the national muffin, the creak of the waiter's shoes as he came and went (could anything be so English as his intensely professional back? it revealed a country of tradition), and the rustle of the newspaper I was too excited to read.

Brian Labone 2000

Liverpool as a city I love. There is only one thing wrong with it – the name. It should be called Everton!

Thursday, 9th October. To our despair; a wet morning, and hopelessly so! At ten o'clock we started in close carriages; Vicky and Bertie with us, the two others in the next carriages. It poured; the roads were a sea of mud, and yet the whole way along was lined with people, and all so wet! The atmosphere was so thick, that we could see a very little way before us. Still, the reception was most enthusiastic. The preparations were beautiful. Liverpool is three miles from Croxteth, but there are houses almost the whole way... I cannot attempt to

describe the route or detail the fine buildings. The streets were densely crowded, in spite of the horrible weather, everything extremely well arranged and beautifully decorated, but the poor people so wet and so dirty! We were obliged to spread Albert's large cloak over us to protect us from the rain and the splashing of the mud.

We drove along part of the Docks, and got out at the place of embarkation, which was covered over; there we went on board the *Fairy*, with our whole party, the Mayor, and gentlemen connected with the Docks and Harbour, and went along all the Docks, which are magnificent. The mass of shipping is quite enormous. We went round the mouth of the Mersey, but could hardly make out anything that was at any distance, and we had all to remain in the Pavilion. We disembarked at the same place, and proceeded to the Town Hall. I must mention here the Seamen's Refuge – a magnificent stone building, of which Albert laid the first stone five years ago. The Town Hall is a very handsome building, beautifully decorated inside, and with fine large rooms. We proceeded to the Council Room, where we stood on a throne and received the addresses of the Mayor and Corporation, to which I read an answer, and then knighted the Mayor, Mr. Bent, a very good man.

We remained nearly half-an-hour afterwards in the Town Hall, as there was too much time, – a rare occurrence. At a little before four we re-entered our carriages, and drove to St. George's Hall, one of the finest of modern buildings. It is worthy of ancient Athens; the elevation is so simple and magnificent. It is well raised, and approached by a splendid flight of steps. We got out here and examined the interior, which is quite unfinished, but will be very fine, – the taste so good and pure... The Law Courts are to be held here, and in the centre is the magnificent Hall, intended for concerts... Albert, who is always so ready to admire whatever is simple and grand, was delighted. He never really admires what is small in purpose and design, what is frittered away in detail, and not chaste and simple...We stepped out in order to gratify the great multitude below. We also appeared on the balcony at the Town Hall.

Quentin Hughes

These slums, viewed romantically, have pictorial qualities – the harsh contrast of blackened brick and a sharp silhouette against those iridescent skies which so characterize the city. Rumpled newsprint lies like a giant white rose on city pavement. The serrated skyline of windowless façades and wet slate roofs in the fleeting light of early morning conjures up a poetry which can be appreciated only by those who do not have to live in these conditions. Nevertheless, these districts of Liverpool have the sharpness of northern wit, the harshness of Lancastrian outspokenness, and occasionally the short-lived beauty which blossoms in a desert.

Reverend James Henley Thornwell 1841

I have arrived here at the finest season of the year. Strawberries and cherries are just ripe, and Liverpool abounds with them. The strawberries are about four times as large as ours. We have also gooseberries in abundance, but they are dreadfully sour. The beef is delicious; and such coffee as I have drunk here I have not tasted in many a day before. In short, so far as my outer man is concerned, I abound in comforts. I have no difficulty in getting along here. I feel perfectly at home. I hear my own language, see many of the customs with which I am familiar, and cannot realize that I am among strangers.

I have been amused here with the warmth with which the people discuss politics. They are just as violent as they are in America. You see handbills stuck up along the streets, by the different parties, just as there was in Columbia, during the contest between Van Buren and Harrison. The tories and whigs are equally violent, and equally abusive. They have public meetings, make furious speeches, abuse the Government, curse one another, generally close by raising a mob, and these are scattered by the police. Another wonder to me, was the prodigious size of the dray horses. They are nearly as large as elephants, very muscular, and two of them draw the weight of six or eight with us. They are too large, however, to be active; and hence I have never seen them move faster than a walk.

John Masefield

The flower of all England's shipping belonged in Liverpool: the river and docks were always busy with the best ships of the time. The Cunard moorings were just downstream from us; the White Star and Inman moorings beyond them; and the P.S.N. and Alfred Holt moorings still further on, but in sight. The Elder Dempster ships were near us in the Sloyne. The steamers of many famous lines were weekly visitors to the river, we knew them all, their funnels, their houseflags and their tenders: even the foreign steamers and what they brought were known to us.

But in those days the bulk of the world's freight was carried in sailing ships, which had then reached their last, strange, beautiful perfection. At all times we could see in the river or in the docks the queens of that last construction, the superb four-masted ships and barques, of from two to three thousand tons, which went with general cargoes to San Francisco and came back with grain. They are now gone, but then they were many; and many of the many were strange with new device of build or rig, of intense interest to us, whose talk and thought was of ships.

Often, perhaps every week, sometimes for weeks together, every day one such queen would come with her tugs into the Sloyne and anchor near us all trim from her last month's work, her sails in harbour-stows, her blocks gleaming, her mainyards still aback, just as they had braced them on taking the towline, and her houseflag at her main truck. Then at the next flood her crowd would man the capstan, her anchor would come in to *Rolling Home* or *Goodbye, fare you well,* and she would pass to dock.

At flood tide in any case the river would waken into bustle and beauty of ships coming in and going out, till it would seem like a street with ships for people. The dock-gates would open to the sound of cheers to let pass some ship with her blue peter flying; barges would tack by under their red sails; schooners, brigantines, yawls and ketches went out or returned, under all sail. Greek and Italian polaccas of all sizes came in under sail. Norwegian barques sometimes sailed in, tack and tack, to anchor near us. No such display of living ships could be seen in any other port in the world at that time.

The display did not cease with the living ships, far from it. On both sides of the river there were the slips and gantries of the building firms, and all the racket and clatter of new construction, always going on in sight and sound of us. We watched ships being built and launched and floated. We saw them going forth in splendour and coming back shattered by the sea, listed, shored up, dismasted, red with sea-rust, white with sea-salt, holed, dinted, ruined, all pumps still spouting, just limping into dock with three tugs, or just crawling to the mud and lying down.

Michael Redgrave   1934

The Liverpool Playhouse theatre had just been redecorated. It was, and is, one of the most attractive old theatres in

England. I saw the matinee, of a play by John Van Druten, and enjoyed it. The company seemed to play to a high standard. But my mind kept wandering to the photographs in front of the theatre. How, I wondered, would mine look amongst them?

Helen Forrester   1940

The huge clock still hangs in Lime Street station, Liverpool, and marks a convenient spot for travellers to be met. During World War II, almost every girl in Liverpool must have written to a serviceman coming home on leave, 'I'll meet you under the clock at Lime Street.' There were always women there, dressed in their shabby best, hair long, curled and glossy, pacing nervously under that indifferent timepiece. Every time a train chugged in, they would glance anxiously at the ticket collectors' wickets, while round them swirled other civilians, and hordes of men and women in uniform, khaki, Navy blue, or Air Force blue, staggering under enormous packs and kitbags. Some men wore foreign uniforms, with shoulder flashes of refugee armies, navies and

air forces. No matter who they were, they all shared the same expression of deep fatigue.

This huge vortex of uprooted humanity was supervised by stolid-looking military police standing like rocks against a tide. Some of them were American Snowdrops, so nicknamed because of their white helmets. Occasionally a single English civilian policeman stood out amongst all the other uniforms, a reminder of peacetime and sanity, when a quiet, 'Now move along there, please,' was enough to reduce a pushing crowd to order.

The station may be rebuilt, the generations pass, but the ghosts are still there, ghosts of lovers, husbands, sons, withered like flowers on distant battlefields long forgotten, and of mothers, wives and sweethearts long since dead. Amongst those kindly shades stands Harry O'Dwyer, the fiancé of my youth, a ship's engineer, lost at sea in 1940.

Ida Wells 1894

But Liverpool has learned that she can prosper without the slave trade or slave labor. Her docks are crowded with ships from all parts of the world. And the city, with its population of six hundred thousand souls, is one of the most prosperous in the United Kingdom. Her freedom-loving citizens not only subscribe to the doctrine that human beings regardless of color or condition are equal before the law, but they practise what they preach.

To a colored person who has been reared in the peculiar atmosphere which obtains only in free (?) America it is like being born into another world, to be welcomed among persons of the highest order of intellectual and social culture as if one were one of themselves.

Here a 'colored' person can ride in any sort of conveyance in any part of the country without being insulted; stop in any hotel or be accommodated at any restaurant one wishes without being refused with contempt; wander into any picture gallery, lecture room, concert hall, theater or church and receive only the most courteous treatment from officials and fellow sightseers. The privilege of being once in a country where 'A man's a man for a' that,' is one which can best be appreciated by those Americans whose black skins are a bar to their receiving genuine kindness and courtesy at home.

Michael Heseltine   1982

The three of us, together with attendant officials, took up residence in the Atlantic Tower Hotel. I was booked into the Port of Liverpool suite on the sixteenth floor and for two and a half weeks this was to be my home. My office during the day was in the Liver Building, the headquarters of the newly established Merseyside Urban Development Corporation.

Alone, every night, when the meetings were over and the pressure was off, I would stand with a glass of wine, looking out at the magnificent view over the river and ask myself what had gone wrong for this great English city. The Mersey, its lifeblood, flowed as majestically as ever down from the hills. Its monumental Georgian and Victorian buildings, created with such pride and at such cost by the city fathers of a century and more earlier, still dominated the skyline. The Liver Building itself, the epicentre of a trading system that had reached out to the four corners of the earth, stood defiant and from my perspective very alone. The port had serviced an empire and sourced a world trade. From Liverpool's docks its ships had plied the seven seas. The quays had been the last stopping place for thousands of fellow countrymen and women and for Europeans of all nations heading for the New World and the gateway for millions of Irish labourers attracted  by work on the railways and canals of England. High above it all loomed the two great cathedrals of Rome and Canterbury, then wedded together in the brotherhood of the Roman Catholic Archbishop Derek Worlock and the Anglican Bishop David Sheppard.

In truth, everything had gone wrong.

Washington Irving   1815

One of the first places to which a stranger is taken in Liverpool is the Athenaeum. It is established on a liberal and judicious plan; it contains a good library, and spacious reading-room, and is the great literary resort of the place. Go there at what hour you may, you are sure to find it filled with grave-looking personages, deeply absorbed in the study of newspapers.

As I was once visiting this haunt of the learned, my attention was attracted to a person just entering the room. He was advanced in life, tall, and of a form that might once have been commanding, but it was a little bowed by time – perhaps by care. He had a noble Roman style of countenance; a head that would have pleased a painter; and though some slight furrows on his brow showed that wasting thought had been busy there, yet his eye still beamed with the fire of a poetic soul. There was something in his whole appearance that indicated a being of a different order from the bustling race around him.

I inquired his name, and was informed that it was Roscoe. I drew back with an involuntary feeling of veneration. This, then, was an author of celebrity: this was one of those men, whose voices have gone forth to the ends of the earth; with whose minds I have communed even in the solitudes of America. Accustomed, as we are in our country, to know European writers only by their works, we cannot conceive of them, as of other men, engrossed by trivial or sordid pursuits, and jostling with the crowd of common minds in the dusty paths of life. They pass before our imaginations like superior beings radiant with the emanations of their own genius, and surrounded by a halo of literary glory.

To find, therefore, the elegant historian of the Medici, mingling among the busy sons of traffic, at first shocked my poetical ideas; but it is from the very circumstances and situation in which he has been placed, that Mr. Roscoe derives his highest claims to admiration. It is interesting to notice how some minds seem almost to create themselves, springing up under every disadvantage, and working their solitary but irresistible way through a thousand obstacles. Nature seems to delight in disappointing the assiduities of art, with which it would rear legitimate dullness to maturity; and to glory in the vigor and luxuriance of her chance productions. She scatters the seeds of genius to the winds, and though some may perish among the stony places of the world, and some be choked by the thorns and brambles of early adversity, yet others will now and then strike root even in the clefts of the rock, struggle bravely up into sunshine, and spread over their sterile birthplace all the beauties of vegetation.

Such has been the case with Mr. Roscoe. Born in a place apparently ungenial to the growth of literary talent; in the very market-place of trade; without fortune, family connections, or patronage; self-prompted, self-sustained, and almost self-taught; he has conquered every obstacle, achieved his way to eminence, and, having become one of the ornaments of the nation, has turned the whole force of his talents and influence to advance and embellish his native town.

John Lennon   1971

My love of New York is something to do with Liverpool. There is the same quality of energy in both cities.

Oliver Lodge   c1885

My time at Luss was interrupted by a promise I had given to the medicals at Liverpool to show some experiments at their

congress and soirée. I had to go all the way back to Liverpool by myself, arriving in the evening, and finding the hotels full, probably for the Grand National. At last I decided to go to our house near Sefton Park, left in the charge of a caretaker; and arriving there very late, I knocked and knocked, but

could gain no admission, I don't believe anyone was in the house. It was too late to do anything else, so I decided to spend the night in Sefton Park. Accordingly I went to the grotto there, and sat on a bench: after a long time of discomfort I went to sleep. When I finally awoke in the morning, a gardener was standing looking at me, leaning on his rake. I gave a jump, and said it was a fine morning – which it wasn't; it was raining. I got away from the park, and went to Isaac Thompson's to see if they would give me breakfast. I arrived for breakfast rather late! This was one of the few times that I have known what it is like to have no place to sleep in. I was left alone, however, in the grotto, and was not moved on by the police.

Thomas De Quincey   c1812

And at that time I often fell into these reveries upon taking opium; and more than once it has happened to me, on a summer night, when I have been at an open window, in a room from which I could overlook the sea at a mile below me, and could command a view of the great town of L--, at about the same distance, that I have sat, from sunset to sunrise, motionless, and without wishing to move.

I shall be charged with mysticism, Behmenism, quietism, &c., but that shall not alarm me. Sir H. Vane, the younger, was one of our wisest men; and let my readers see if he, in his philosophical works, be half as unmystical as I am. I say, then, that it has often struck me that the scene itself was somewhat typical of what took place in such a reverie. The town of L-- represented the earth, with its sorrows and its graves left behind, yet not out of sight, nor wholly forgotten.

The ocean, in everlasting but gentle agitation, and brooded over by a dove-like calm, might not unfitly typify the mind and the mood which then swayed it. For it seemed to me as if then first I stood at a distance, and aloof from the uproar of life; as if the tumult, the fever, and the strife, were suspended; a respite granted from the secret burdens of the heart; a sabbath of repose; a resting from human labours. Here were the hopes which blossom in the paths of life, reconciled with the peace which is in the grave; motions of the intellect as unwearied as the heavens, yet for all anxieties a halcyon calm; a tranquility that seemed no product of inertia, but as if resulting from mighty and equal antagonisms; infinite activities, infinite repose.

Margaret Cole   1911

I could not altogether fail to notice the Liverpool Dock Strike. I remember a broiling August, so hot that a piece of chocolate laid on a chair by Ray's bedside – he had heart trouble and was fainting with the heat – itself fainted and dropped limply towards the floor. I remember the stench of the unscavenged streets – the Corporation employees came out in sympathy – and of the truckloads of vegetables rotting at Edge Hill station. I remember bits of broken bottle, relics of battles down by the Docks, the rain-patter of feet walking the pavements when the trams ceased to run and clank, the grey *Antrim* lying on guard in the Mersey, the soldiers marching through the streets, special editions of the evening papers coming out every half-hour, and American tourists, decanted from the *Baltic*, sitting at Pier Head on their Saratoga trunks with no porters to carry them away. I gathered from my father's thunderous noises that it was the beginning of the end of the world; but as to what it was all about I had not the slightest idea – I had to read my husband's first book to find out.

Joseph Conrad ✒ 1920

Dear Mr Holt.

To be still recognised, after all these years, as a seaman by the head of a House known so long and so highly honoured on the wide seas touches me deeply. I wish to thank you warmly for a moment of sincere emotion of a kind I did not think life could yet hold for me in store.

I will confess to you my diffidence – as a man of the port of London honoured by being called into counsel on a Liverpool scheme. In your great Sea-City, which always has been regarded in my time as the premier port of the United Kingdom, you have round you all the assistance that experience, knowledge and native sagacity can give.

Lydia Sigourney 1840

It is impossible to listen without emotion to the sacred music of the blind, in their Church at Liverpool. They chant as in the cathedral-service, accompanied by the organ, and sing anthems and other compositions with a soul-thrilling sweetness. Of course, all these performances are acts of memory, which is doubtless rendered more retentive by the concentrativeness of thought, which blindness promotes. The noble Asylum for these sightless worshippers is well patronized. Their Church is adorned with two large paintings, and a transparency; and was filled by a respectable audience. The seats for the objects of the Institution are in the gallery. Sweet and heaven-born is that Charity, which, if she may not like her Master open the blind eye to the works of nature, pours upon the afflicted mind the light of knowledge, and lifts up the soul to the 'clear shining of the sun of righteousness'.

We were taken by the kindness of a friend to the after-noon worship in the Chapel of the Blue Coat Hospital. Two hundred and fifty boys, and one hundred girls, were assem-bled there, in the neat uniforms of the Institution. To our surprise the whole service was performed by them. A boy of very grave deportment read the liturgy with a solemn intonation, and the others distinctly responded. Another officiated as organist, and all joined zealously in the singing. Catechisms and portions of Scripture were recited by a selection of the scholars, and the exercises conducted and closed decorously.

The building appropriated to the Institution is spacious, and perfectly neat. In one apartment are portraits of its benefactors, among whom are some, who were once pension-ers of its bounty. The advantages for an extended education are not so great here, as in the establishment for the Blue Coat Boys in London, which has produced some literary men of note. The Liverpool beneficiaries are prepared for the practi-cal walks of life, and become apprentices to artisans, or tradesmen. Before leaving, we were invited to see the children taking their Sunday supper. Each had on a wooden plate a huge mass of bread, with a modicum of cheese, and by its side a small cup of ale; all of which elements they were discussing with a visible relish. Their appearance was healthful, and their deportment quiet, and in perfect subordination. How true is that benevolence, which rescues the young from ignorance and poverty, and inspires them with motives to become useful here, and happy hereafter. It is peculiarly honorable in a commercial city, to devote time and attention to these departments of philanthropy.

Edwin Lutyens   1936

For days I have been miz – sleepless. I don't think I told you.

The Liverpool Cath committee had been on their hind legs, and for a second time commanded me to push on with the Cathedral and leave out all granite, like asking you whilst knitting me a pair of woollen socks 'get on – omit all wool!' The Arch was perfectly furious squashed the committee and supported me so once again I breathed, and all is well.

Julian Cope   1977

It was freezing. January 1977 in Liverpool was ice and wind. The Damned were playing Eric's in two days. I went to an Army & Navy and got my first drainpipe jeans for a pound. They were in a skip on the ground floor full of jeans and pink

T-shirts. The T-shirts were 30p so I bought one. Back at college, I wondered what to wear. Brian lent me a leather jacket and at least I had drainies, but my hair was still shit. Maybe we'd be the coolest. Ho-hum.

Eric's club was in Mathew Street, opposite where the Cavern used to be. Next to it was a pub called the Grapes where everyone went. You'd go there before Eric's but we didn't know this yet. The Grapes was full of scene characters that I wanted to know. One day. But now I was a nervous farm-punk and everyone seemed a million miles away.

Frederick Law Olmsted   1850

The baker had begged of us not to leave Birkenhead without seeing their new park, and at his suggestion we left our knapsacks with him, and proceeded to it. As we approached the entrance, we were met by women and girls, who, holding out a cup of milk, asked us – *'Will you take a cup of milk, sirs? – good, cool, sweet cow's milk, gentlemen, or right warm from the ass!'* And at the gate was a herd of donkeys, some with cans of milk strapped to them, others saddled and bridled, to be let for ladies and children to ride.

The gateway, which is about a mile and a half from the ferry, and quite back of the town, is a great, massive block of handsome Ionic architecture, standing alone, and unsupported by any thing else in the vicinity, and looking, as I think, heavy and awkward. There is a sort of grandeur about it that the English are fond of, but which, when it is entirely separate from all other architectural constructions, always strikes me unpleasantly. It seems intended as an impressive preface to a great display of art within; but here, as well as at

Eaton Park, and other places I have since seen, it is not followed up with great things, the grounds immediately within the grand entrance being simple, and apparently rather overlooked by the gardener. There is a large archway for carriages, and two smaller ones for those on foot, and, on either side, and over these, are rooms, which probably serve as inconvenient lodges for the laborers. No porter appears, and the gates are freely opened to the public.

Walking a short distance up an avenue, we passed through another light iron gate into a thick, luxuriant, and diversified garden. Five minutes of admiration, and a few more spent studying the manner in which art had been employed to obtain from nature so much beauty, and I was ready to admit that in democratic America there was nothing to be thought of as comparable with this People's Garden. Indeed, gardening, had here reached a perfection that I had never before dreamed of. I cannot undertake to describe the effect of so much taste and skill as had evidently been employed; I will only tell you, that we passed by winding paths, over acres and acres, with a constant varying surface, where on all sides were growing every variety of shrubs and flowers, with more than natural grace, all set in borders of greenest, closest turf, and all kept with most consummate neatness. At a distance of a quarter of a mile from the gate, we came to an open field of clean, bright, green-sward, closely mown, on which a large tent was pitched, and a party of boys in on one part, and a party of gentlemen in another, were playing cricket. Beyond this was a large meadow with rich groups of trees, under which a flock of sheep were reposing, and girls and women with children, were playing. While watching the cricketers, we were threatened with a shower, and hastened to look for shelter, which we found in a pagoda, on an island approached by a Chinese bridge. It was soon filled, as were the other ornamental buidlings, by a crowd of those who, like ourselves, had been overtaken in the grounds by the rain; and I was glad to observe that the privileges of the garden were enjoyed equally by all classes.

James Scott Walker   1830

About two thirds of the tunnel is driven through the solid rock, and where that was found defective, owing to slips in the formation, or where sand, clay, or slaty and insecure material had to be perforated, the whole is strongly arched with brick. Stone was at first employed, but the size of the blocks being found to be inconvenient for working on the centres, brick-work of 18 inches to two feet in thickness was adopted, and is adequate to every purpose of strength and neatness. The gradual and careful manner in which the archwork has been turned is observable on the roof, – on which may be traced the junction of each successive span, of about a yard in breadth, as the workmen were enabled to move the centre forward for its support. During the operations, the writer of this frequently visited the several points of excavation, and never without impressions of wonder and admiration. In the compact rock, the roof and sides were first sought or scooped out, the middle serving as standing ground for the workmen, to be gradually removed as they proceeded. The manner of working through the softer materials, where water was often met with, was necessarily more cautious, and in some parts was attended with difficulties which were at first discouraging, but which the Engineer and his assistants surmounted by skill and perseverance. Seen and heard from a distance through the intermediate darkness, the labour of the miners was truly interesting. Their numerous candles twinkled in the thick obscurity like stars on a gloomy night, and their figures here and there marked out in dark profile, while they flung about their brawny arms, – together with the frequent explosion and the fumes of gunpowder, conveyed no contemptible idea of some infernal operation in the regions of Pluto.

Frederick Gibberd   1968

In the atmosphere of Liverpool there is little of the bright sun and hard, clear light that made possible the precision of form and silhouette of the classic architecture of Greece and Rome. The atmosphere tends to be diffused and ethereal; the sun, if it appears at all, struggles through a haze of clouds. It has always seemed to me that the spiky silhouette of the Gothic cathedral mingles perfectly with the atmosphere of the Gothic North; rather than leave the tower as a rigid geometric form I diffused the silhouette by a structure of pinnacles.

Ann Maury   1846

July 30th. After resting awhile Rutson & I walked out to the Dingle & there took tea with a large party under the Tent in the field. About the same time some of the gentlemen of the family went to dine with the Prince at the Town Hall. The Banquet there did not go off so well as the earlier one. When dinner was all ready to be put upon the table, there was a strike for wages amongst the waiters, & it took so long to adjust the differences between the high contending parties that it was a quarter before 9 when dinner was announced. The provisions were spoken of as being badly cooked & deficient in quantity. The Prince did not leave the table until midnight. Fire works were to be seen in great beauty as we returned from the Dingle.

31st July 1846. Another brilliant day, the sun shining in full radiance. Rutson and I set out at 11 o'clock to go to the Sailors Home, or at least to the site for it, there to await the ceremony of laying the first stone. We walked along Berry St. & saw about 1000 children ranged on the steps of St. Luke's Church Yard, an admirable position from which to see the procession, from its gradual elevation and occupying a corner which overlooked 2 streets. Though the shops in Bold St. & Church St. were closed yet it presented a most animated scene. The shop windows were most of them filled with pretty & well dressed young women seated on gradually rising benches so as to see well to the very back. The windows & doors tastefully ornamented with festoons & emblematical devices wreaths of flowers etc. etc. & in some instances triumphal arches stretched across the street.

The footways were occupied by men, women & children who had already taken position to see the show. At the cross streets carts were backed filled with persons paying a piece for the place. Every vacant spot of ground had its platform full of spectators. We walked slowly down admiring the varied scene by the way. As we approached the Custom House the street was kept open by policemen & a troop of soldiers were stationed near the entrance to the enclosure. We were admitted on presenting our tickets & placed ourselves very well near the scarlet cloth laid down for the Prince to stand upon. It was a wearisome business waiting so many hours basking in the hot sun without any awning. Occasionally there was a little variety from some disorderly proceeding in the crowd. A man was thrown out of the Custom House window, & tumbled over and over on the heads of the multitude apparently unhurt. When the procession arrived a small number of the Blue Coat boys were admitted & small numbers of each society. The space was limited & more were desirous of getting in than had been arranged, & quarelling followed between the police & the Reckabites & it seemed as if mischief must follow from so much anger, blows having already been given. At this moment Lord Adolphus Fitz Clarence went to the excited men, & harangued them so skillfully that he restored order & good humour & was exceedingly cheered.

Phil Jones 1989

Well, I didn't go to Hillsborough. I wasn't one of the ones who'd go to a game without a ticket like a lot of my friends would, if I didn't get a ticket I wouldn't go. But it affected me – it did affect me massively. I mean, I think it's a strange one, I don't like to sort of say it 'cos you feel like you're takin' away from the people who were actually involved, but I think I actually sort of suffered with depression shortly after that. I have been treated with depression and stuff.

That day when it happened I was sittin' in my house, my mum's house it was at that point, with my mate upstairs and we were listenin' to it on the radio. The reports were comin' through about fans on the pitch, that's all it was sayin' at the time, there was no hint of a crush or nothin'. The telly was on in the room and we could see quite clearly it wasn't a pitch invasion as in a violent pitch invasion, it was people tryin' to drag people out and you could see right from the start what was goin' on, but almost immediately I started making like a mental list in my mind then of people I knew – it was between 200 and 300.

Words can't describe how bad that day was. I was ringing round as many people as I could 'Have you heard from this?', so I was ringing their parents and they'd go 'Yeah, he's rang he's okay', or whatever, you know. It got to about 11 o'clock when the final person that we were tryin' to contact we made contact with, which was Dosher. But by that point there was about 10 people that come round who'd been the game as well and come round to my house to tell me what was goin' on and all that.

We all just sort of sat and drank and talked about it, it

didn't really hit home. Still we all got up the next mornin' to go down the cathedral – I don't even know why we knew we would do that. We just sort of got up and we were at the bus stop and there was people doin' the same thing. We all just congregated outside the cathedral, everyone was in shock. I mean people didn't – people weren't speakin', there was thousands of people just walkin' round just not speakin', it was weird.

Carla Lane   2002

As a child I always loved Speke Hall near Liverpool where I grew up and I used to take my children there – I have a deep seated love for it and I often think I fell for my manor because it reminded me of Speke Hall. It's a haunting place and all through my life I've found myself driving back there.

Hans Caspar Escher   1814

On Sunday, August 21, we left Manchester and reached Liverpool at three o'clock in the afternoon. Sunday is kept very strictly in English towns so that all that we could do (when we got to Liverpool) was to take a walk through the town and the harbour which was full of ships. That quarter of Liverpool which is next to the docks consists of many warehouses which are eight or nine storeys high. Since Manchester – and indeed Lancashire – are covered with countless spinning mills Liverpool is the port which handles all the American cotton destined for this industrial area. Many types of cotton, which we never see in Switzerland are sold in Liverpool. Here, for example, the merchants deal in four to five different types of Georgia *longue soie*.

The district between Manchester and Liverpool is well culti-vated. In the vicinity of Liverpool I saw more fruit trees than I saw around London. Here people eagerly eat quite green apples with white kernels that in Switzerland would only be fed to the pigs. In all English towns one sees the finest hot-house grapes from Madeira and other places in the warm zone but they lack the fresh aroma that is the mark of grapes which have been grown in the open.

Liverpool is a fairly well planned town. As in London most buildings are constructed with red bricks but there are some buildings in which reddish and yellow sandstone has been used. In Liverpool, as in other English towns, there are many

churches – and other new public build-ings – which have been constructed in the gothic style which has a pleasing effect.

I visited one of the many factories making ships' ropes which are to be found in Liverpool. The machinery in these works was one of the most remark-able things that I have seen so far in England. The machinery in a cotton mill is insignificant when compared with the machinery in a rope works. This ropery had five floors and a basement. All the machinery was driven by a 24 horse power steam engine. The building had 15 windows in a row (on each floor). Very few workers are needed to operate the machinery. There is no danger of the rope breaking and having to be repaired.

The institute for the blind – in which a considerable

number of blind people of both sexes and various ages are accommodated and usefully employed – has been erected and is maintained by public subscription. This accords with normal English practice. The small facade of the institute facing the street is built in a simple fashion. The rooms occupied by the supervisor are situated in this part of the building. Behind these rooms is a very large courtyard around which are situated the dining rooms, the bedrooms, and the various workshops of the inmates. All the rooms are linked by the narrow paved corridors. On each side of a corridor there is a row of thin cast iron pillars which are linked by rails made of cast iron.

John Shaw   1861

The unusual amount of Irish resident in Liverpool, many of them grossly ignorant, tends not a little to make the place worse than it otherwise would be. I worked with the missionary in Naylor Street and St. Paul's Street, where they chiefly reside. The chief of them are Roman Catholics, and being grossly ignorant, many of them are incapable of either reading or writing, entertain a strong distaste for Protestantism. Upon one occasion, a man was killed very near to Naylor Street. He was literally stoned to death! Such was the fear created in the minds of those who beheld this atrocious murder, that for a considerable time no one dare approach the murdered man. At another time, a Protestant was overheard by some Catholics talking about his religion in some pot-house. On his quitting the place, the Catholics way-laid him, attacked him, and half-killed him, by jumping on him. The young people are not a whit better than the old, for whenever a Protestant and a Catholic school meet, they are sure to attack each other: the Catholics, I am informed, are generally the aggressors.

In walking down one of these streets where these miserable people reside, accompanied by the missionary, a poor woman stepped hurriedly out of a house just before us, staggering and reeling under the influence of a perhaps fatal blow, which she had just received. The blood was streaming from both ears, proving the danger as well as the power of the blow. The missionary did not busy himself to enquire at the house from whence she came, the cause of this brutal attack, most probably from fear of coming in contact with some one who might not hesitate to serve him out by a similar attack for his impertinence and inquisitiveness. Nor did he deem it prudent to follow her, which very much surprised me at the time.

Annie Forshaw   1860

Lodge Lane in 1860 was a picturesque country lane, bordered with white thorn hedges; old Georgian houses

stood on one side; on the other, pretty little white cottages. At the foot of the garden of No.33, Grove Park, near a big ash tree was a small but deep pond, a little beyond which used to stand in line the targets of the *Mersey Bowmen*. The Archery Ground extended southwards approximately to the site of the present houses of Croxteth Grove, whilst to mark the Western boundary four trees were planted near the Lodge Lane footpath. The stumps of these trees may be seen to-day in front of the house of Colonel Albert Melly which stands on the site of the old archery ground.

In 1865 the Club changed its ground, moving northwards up Lodge Lane to a new site now occupied by the houses on the north side of Coltart Road.

In those days 'Coltart's Ropery' was there and the south border of the archery ground was formed by the back of the sheds of the Rope Walk. Standing at the Lodge Lane end of the Rope Walk was the house of Mr. William A. Jevons, a well-known Liverpool Solicitor, through whose stable yard the members of the *Mersey Bowmen* used to enter the Archery Ground.

From this ground behind the sheds of Coltart's Rope Walk the *Mersey Bowmen* again moved, in 1867 or 1868, and established their headquarters on the farm at the corner of Ullet Road and Lodge Lane (now Sefton Park Road), of which the lessee was then Mr. Thomas Aspinall.

There they remained until 1872.

Jack Kerouac   1943

Then we sailed down into the Irish Sea, laid anchor off Belfast, waited there for some British convoy boats, and crossed the Irish Sea that afternoon and night straight for Liverpool. 1943. The year the Beatles were born there, ha ha ha.

And the year some little bum in a derby hat took my advice and lived with his legs whole. As we came up the Mersey River, all mud brown, and turned in to an old wooden dock, there was a little fellow of Great Britain waving a newspaper at me and yelling, about 100 yards ahead as we bore directly on him. He had his bicycle beside him. Finally I could see he was yelling something about 'Yank! Hey Yank! There's been a great Allied victory in Salerno! Did ye know that?'

'I dont know, Mr English, but please get off that pier, from what I can tell we're going to ram it down head on...' But he couldnt hear me because of the wind and the tide and the noise of cranes and winches unloading the ships nearby on the Merseyside docks.

'Yank! Yank!'

'But, mon' – I think the captain'd gotten drunk at last for the first time and the chief mate maybe too on Schnapps – 'but please turn around and start running as fast as you can, this ship is not going to touch at that dock, it's going to ram it! The bridge is drunk!'

'Hey? Hey what? Salerno!'

I kept waving him away. I pointed at the bow, the bridge, the dock, at him, I said 'Run run run... away!' He took off his derby hat and ran back with his bike he was pushing, and sure enough, the bow of the S.S. *George Weems* carrying 500-pound bombs and flying the red dynamite flag rammed right into that rotten old wood wharf and completely demolished it, ce-rack-ke-rack-crack, timbers, wood planks, nails, old rat nests, a mess of junk all upended like with a bulldozer and we came to a stop in Great Britain.

'This sceptred isle.'

Now, if it had been a modern concrete job, goodbye Du

Louse, this book, the whole crew and nothing but the crew, and 'alf and 'alf of Liverpool.

******

Where does a Captain go when his ship's finally docked and here he comes out after supper all decked out in his best suit, with epaulets and all, and steps down the gangplank carefully to a waiting cab or limousine? And in this here wartime Liverpool, was he about to go have dinner (cocktails first) in a castle over a sea-crashin cliff? Or a lounge somewhere? In fact, and where does the scarred first mate go with his snarling smear of thoughts, to weirder friends somewhere? In fact, and where, even, the bosun, the lowest Portuguese ordinary, the engine room, where do they go? They're all togged out and stepping out? They amaze me as I watch them go. Because I've agreed to work the whole weekend for the Portuguese ordinary so that when he comes back, I myself can have two straight days in a row. Anybody wondering what *I'm* going to do? But where do captains go? It's like wondering about where elephants go when they die, with their tusks. Some hidden blonde? Some old fishy Britisher seadog friend who taught him to read maps in Magellan rooms? I don't care if the port's Norfolk Virginia or Liverpool or Hong Kong they must surely go to strange places. So I'm there watching everybody going ashore, I have to stay aboard two days and fiddle with the loading spotlights and the wires that feed them with electricity, make coffee for the gangplank watch, and in the morning watch all those crazy little Liverpudlian longshoremen come rushing up on their bicycles with their lunches and their thermos bottles of 'tay' as they eagerly get down to the 'job' of unloading those awesome big 500-pound bombs destined for poor old sweet Dresden or someplace of Hamburg.

But that first night, a Friday, practically the whole crew gone, I wheedled the lines around, put up rat guards extra against the original ones, pointed the spotlights right, made coffee, and mostly spent most of my time rearranging things on deck and saying to myself 'Aye saye, Mayeteee' in imitation of the Lancashire accents of the longshoremen. My nose was sniffling in the riverside cool, I was having fun, all alone practically on one big ship, and suddenly it began to occur to me that someday I would become a real serious writer with no time to fool around with poetry or form or style. Besides, at dusk, red on the Mersey liquid belly, here goes this oldest and littlest freighter I ever saw in my life with old fellas sitting on the afterdeck in old chairs smoking out of pipes, the S.S. *Long Voyage Home*, bound for Bangkok I guess for the thousandth time, the ship just slipping past me at my rail, the old men not looking up, just a touch away, by pole anyway, into the sinking sun they go on long voyages to the Pacific: and I'm wondering 'Joseph Conrad wasnt wrong, there *are* old seadogs who've been to everywhere from Bombay to British Columbia smoking their pipes on poops of old sea vessels, practically born at sea they are, and die at sea, and dont even look up... Even have cats down below for the rats, and sometimes a dog...What tobacco they smoke? What they do, where they go when they put on their glad rags in old Macao, to do what? What a vast crock it all is for me to even dare to think of anything when all is said and done, Mayetey, I saye, get those lines wound right...' Talking to myself, I laughed all night. Not even a drink since Brooklyn...

Who needs it?

Maybe at noon I'd slip off down the cobblestoned Merseyside streets and try the pub, it was always closed, not alone they didnt have any sausage in wartime England except was made with sawdust, but no beer proper either. And always closed. Some bold old bum in a bar complained that the poor of Liverpool were using their bathtubs to put coal in.

But when my weekend was over and Portugee came back to take over my duties for two days, I put on MY glad rags, which was a shiny oiled black leather jacket, khaki shirt, black tie, Merchant Marine Army Navy Store phony goldbraid hat 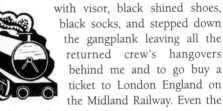 with visor, black shined shoes, black socks, and stepped down the gangplank leaving all the returned crew's hangovers behind me and to go buy a ticket to London England on the Midland Railway. Even the captain was back now, disappointed I'm sure.

I got a haircut downtown Liverpool, hung around the rail station, the USO club looking at magazines and pingpong players, rain, the rimed old monuments by the quai, pigeons, and the train across strange smokepots of Birkenhead and into the heart of *La Grande Bretagne* ('the Great Britain').

Liverpool Review   1891

The mosque is a large room, which on this occasion had an Eastern appearance, the windows being draped with rich Burmese curtains and the floor carpeted with bright Turkish rugs.

Punctually at the appointed time the bridal party entered the mosque and at once formed themselves into a semi-circle. The bride, who has reached her thirty-first year and is a charming lady, is the eldest daughter of the late Mr. Charles Fitch, J.P., of London. She was accompanied by her brother and two ladies, and wore a light grey cloth dress trimmed with broad gold braid; her hat, with pale grey ostrich feathers and gold braid trimming, being to match. The bridegroom is a Mohammedan gentleman and a barrister-at-law practising in the metropolis, and his father, the Nawab Vicarul Muilk Bahadur, is the financial secretary to the Nizam of Hyderabad. He is twenty-four years of age, of bronzed complexion, and the ladies were struck by his exceedingly handsome appearance. He wore a sort of officer's undress uniform of black cloth and was accompanied by Mr. Quilliam.

When the semi-circle was formed the officiating member of the congregation advanced to read the service, which was conducted in Arabic and English. On this occasion it was Mr. R. Almad, the vice-president, who bore the title of *moulvie*, or one learned in the Arabic tongue, for there are no ministers among the Moslems, all the members with the lingual qualifications being entitled to officiate.

It may be mentioned, parenthetically, that the bride is a Christian lady, and after several clergymen had refused to perform the Christian ceremony of marriage, it was ultimately celebrated at St. Giles', Camberwell. There was a Christian clergyman present on Saturday but he desired that his name should not be given.

The *moulvie* wore a gorgeous costume consisting of a long

robe of crimson silk, with dark green lining, beneath which was a tight-fitting tunic of embroidered black velvet, and a broad and ornamented golden belt. His turban was of white silk. The service began by simply asking the consent of the two persons principally interested. This received, the bride repeated after the *moulvie*, in English, 'I stand here in the presence of God, and all of you who are assembled here, to unite my heart to your heart, and my destiny to your destiny, and to be called by thy name.' She also vowed to be 'an affectionate and constant wife, and to stand faithfully by thy side, whether in health or sickness, whether in prosperity or adversity; and thy sorrow shall be my sorrow, and thy happiness shall be my happiness'. The bridegroom said, following the *moulvie*, in Arabic and English, 'I stand here this day to make with thee a covenant of affection and truth, and to take thee, Charlotte Fitch, to be my wedded wife... I shall cherish thee according to the means with which God shall bless me; thy sorrow shall be my sorrow, and thy happiness shall be my happiness.'

Maria Mitchell

I have been to visit Mr. Lassell. He called yesterday and asked me to dine with him to-day. He has a charming place, about four miles out of Liverpool; a pretty house and grounds.

Mr. Lassell has constructed two telescopes, both on the Newtonian plan; one of ten, the other of twenty, feet in length. Each has its separate building, and in the smaller building is a transit instrument.

Mr. Lassell must have been a most indefatigable worker as well as a most ingenious man; for, besides constructing his own instruments, he has found time to make discoveries. He is, besides, very genial and pleasant, and told me some good anecdotes connected with astronomical observations.

One story pleased me very much. Our Massachusetts astronomer, Alvan Clark, has long been a correspondent of Mr. Dawes, but has never seen him. Wishing to have an idea of his person, and being a portrait painter, Mr. Clark sent to Mr. Dawes for his daguerreotype, and from that painted a likeness, which he has sent out to Liverpool, and which is said to be excellent.

Mr. Lassell looks in at the side of his reflecting telescopes by means of a diagonal eye-piece; when the instrument is pointed at objects of high altitude he hangs a ladder upon the dome and mounts; the ladder moves around with the dome. Mr. Lassell works only for his own amusement, and has been to Malta, – carrying his larger telescope with him, – for the sake of clearer skies. Neither Mr. Lassell nor Mr. Hartnup makes regular observations.

The Misses Lassell, four in number, seem to be very accomplished. They take photographs of each other which are beautiful, make their own picture-frames, and work in the same workshop with their father. One of them told me that she made observations on my comet, supposing it to belong to Mr. Dawes, who was a friend of hers.

They keep an album of the autographs of their scientific visitors, and among them I saw those of Professor Young, of Dartmouth, and of Professor Loomis.

August 4. I have just returned from a visit to the Liverpool Observatory, under the direction of Mr. Hartnup. It is situated on Waterloo dock, and the pier of the observatory rests upon the sandstone of that region. The telescope is an equatorial; like many good instruments in our country, it is almost unused.

Mr. Hartnup's observatory is for nautical purposes. I found him a very gentlemanly person, and very willing to show me anything of interest about the observatory; but they make no regular series of astronomical observations, other than those required for the commerce of Liverpool.

Mr. Hartnup has a clock which by the application of an electric current controls the action of other clocks, especially

the town clock of Liverpool – distant some miles. The current of electricity is not the motive power, but a corrector.

Much attention is paid to meteorology. The pressure of the wind, the horizontal motion, and the course are recorded upon sheets of paper running upon cylinders and connected with the clock; the instrument which obeys the voice of the wind being outside.

John Betjeman 1970

This is one of the great buildings of the world... The impression of vastness, strength and height no words can describe... Suddenly, one sees that the greatest art of architecture, that lifts one up and turns one into a king, yet compels reverence, is the art of enclosing space.

John James Audubon 1826

When I arrived in this city I felt dejected, yes miserably so. The uncertainty of being kindly received, of having my work approved, were all acting on both my physical and mental powers. I felt as if nutritive food within my sight was not to be touched. Now how different my sensations! I am well received wherever I am known. Every object known to me smiles as I meet it, and my poor heart is at last relieved the great anxiety that has for so many years agitated it, by the feeling that I have not worked altogether in vain: that I may no longer be positively ashamed of the production of my pencil.

Otto Frisch c1940

I remember one occasion when he had arranged for me to

play the piano to a group of Polish soldiers stationed in Liverpool. When I got there I found a classroom with something like a hundred people crammed into it, and an old upright piano with half a dozen keys not working. One trial  made me give up the idea of playing any delicate tune, which would be ruined if one note didn't come through; I would have to play music consisting largely of octaves and making a lot of noise. Indeed I had the cheek to play Chopin's *Grande Polonaise*, really far too difficult for me. But to those Poles, I still think it meant a lot. For them the *Grande Polonaise* is almost like a National Anthem, and to hear it played in a foreign land was a rousing experience; there was a storm of applause when I had finished my very ragged performance.

Elizabeth Davis Bancroft   1846

I like these people in Liverpool. They seem to me to think less of fashion and more of substantial excellence than our wealthy people. I am not sure but the existence of a higher class above them has a favorable effect, by limiting them in some ways. There is much less show of furniture in the houses than with us, though their servants and equipages are in much better keeping. I am not sorry to be detained here for a few days by my illness to become acquainted with them, and I think your father likes it also, and will find it useful to him. Let me say, while I think of it, how much I was pleased with the *Great Western*. That upper saloon with the air passing through it was a great comfort to me. The captain, the servants, the table, are all excellent. Everything on board was as nice as in the best hotel, and my gruels and broths beautifully made. One of the stewardesses did more for me than I ever had done by any servant of my own... Your father and Louisa were ill but three or four days, and then your father read Tacitus and talked to the ladies, while Louisa played with the other children.

The Adelphi, my first specimen of an English hotel, is perfectly comfortable, and though an immense establishment, is quiet as a private house. There is none of the bustle of the Astor, and if I ring my bedroom bell it is answered by a woman who attends to me assiduously. The landlord pays us a visit every day to know if we have all we wish.

Matthew Arnold 1882

My darling
Dick saw me off in the rain; at Liverpool I left my things at the station and drove to Rodney Street. There was a champagne luncheon for about 30, chiefly doctors, but you know I like doctors. Then Dr Glynn drove me, in the rain again, to St George's Hall, where we found Lord Derby. There were 1200 people present, I am told – at any rate the Hall was quite full. Lord Derby covered me with compliments, and I was very well received.

Agnes Cowper 1915

On arriving at Birkenhead a scene of unusual activity presented itself. Newspaper boys, bearing the latest news placards before them were dashing up and down the platforms selling their papers while knots of people stood eagerly scanning the lists of survivors reported therein; others were loudly denouncing the nation that had designed and carried into practice so vile a plot against helpless and innocent people. The ferrysteamer was unusually crowded with passengers of every description who, on disembarking at Liverpool, proceeded, almost without exception, direct to the Cunard offices, then in Water Street. I joined this company for I wanted to take home the latest reports. The offices were besieged with anxious enquirers, for everyone in that throng had somebody for whom they cared on board the *Lusitania*, either as passenger or, as in the majority of cases, member of the crew. Members of this great gathering were very orderly and subdued as they worked their way into the enquiry room. They appeared to be stunned by the immensity of the crime and although a few received glad tidings of those dear to them, the great majority turned sadly away to await further news. I was informed there was no word yet of my brother or his travelling companion. Heavy-hearted I reached home. My mother was sitting alone and as I entered the room she looked up and sadly exclaimed, 'Nancie, history repeats itself.' My mind was instantly thrown back to that memorable day, twenty years previously, when news came of my father's loss at sea.

We did not retire, for sleep would have been impossible. We were doing our best to convince each other that the morrow would bring good news when, at one a.m., came a ring at the bell, and mother cried, 'Thank God, he is safe.' And sure enough, there in the doorway stood a telegraph messenger holding the familiar orange-coloured envelope which held the message, 'Saved, Ernest.' A short time ago I had the occasion to search among my mother's papers and found this telegram put carefully away. It was evidently one of her family treasures.

On the following morning I arrived at the Dingle Station of the Overhead Railway, where it came as a great surprise to me to be confronted with the large newspaper placard of a well-known pictorial daily bearing a picture of my brother Ernest holding a small child whom, as I later learned from the paper, he had been instrumental in saving from the wreck. Later in the day another telegram arrived, saying, 'Will arrive Sunday five fifteen Woodside Station.'

*****

At last the train was signalled; a silence, weird and awesome, fell upon us broken only by the voice of a little child calling 'Want to go home mummy, want to go home.' I saw the Salvationist relieve the woman of her infant; and then the  train came steaming in. Oh! The mingled joy and agony of the next few seconds as carriage doors were flung open giving back, as from the dead, a few, but alas, for that tragic group, not one. Then a woman's voice was heard calling, 'Has no one seen my Jim?' The returned survivors were greeted in silence by their friends who, in the face of so much stark sorrow, seemed to realise that audible expressions of their own great joy would be hardly less an outrage. My brother was caught and held by women who eagerly accosted him with such questions as 'Mister, did you see a big tall man anywhere; my husband?'

The train soon emptied of its comparatively few survivor occupants among whom the members of that poor, stricken group of women sought in vain for even one familiar face. At this moment an official of the Cunard Company was observed by them and was implored to say when and where the next batch of survivors would arrive. I found myself straining anxiously for the reply. The official hesitated but finally, with an effort, braced himself to say, 'No more; no more. It is much better for you to know the truth; there are no more to come, not one.' Then a low chorus of moans arose from the tortured watchers who at last realised that nevermore would they behold the loved form of husband, father or son.

*****

Late that evening, in the Scotland Road district of Liverpool severe anti-German riots broke out, led by seamen and dockers who had lost relatives or friends, and by others who had worked aboard 'Lusie', the pride of the port, and whose dastardly end they were determined to avenge. So an infuriated mob set out and proceeded to sack and destroy premises occupied by Germans and Austrians. Windows were smashed, furniture destroyed and stocks were flung into the streets. The city police with mounted constabulary made an effort to cope with the situation, but the mob successfully continued its trail of destruction for several hours. As is so often the case, the innocent, in many instances, suffered for the guilty, for many of the victims of the attack had been citizens of Liverpool for the better part of their lives, living peaceably and industriously among its people.

Courtney Love 1982

If Liverpool was a person I woulndt sleep with it.

Eric Thomas Svedenstierna 1803

Liverpool, which is now regarded as the largest commercial town in Great Britain after London, is probably, in respect of its extent and population, one of the most important in the whole world. Its commerce has in a space of 15 to 20 years so noticeably increased that whereas Bristol, whose trade may be somewhat in decline, formerly had twice as much commerce as Liverpool, the proportions are now said to be reversed. This is attributed in part to the position, which is very advantageous for overseas trade, for communications with Ireland, and for the commission and transportation business with the large inland manufacturing towns; and in part it is seen as a consequence of the generally recognised industry, mode of living, and thrift of the inhabitants. The harbour here, which is good in itself, has been made more convenient in recent times by means of docks and landing stages, and one needs only to be there for a short time to get an approximate idea of the quantity of goods loaded and unloaded, of the numbers of arriving and departing ships, and of the
value of the enormous stocks which
are in the warehouse near the
harbour.

Already the West Indian trade, in

which Liverpool competes even with London, may well demand an unbelievably large capital; for besides seventy or more slave ships, which are annually sent to the African coast, and afterwards take rich cargoes to the West Indies, several small vessels are engaged in this trade. Also I saw here cotton, coffee, and sugar being unloaded in the same quantities as are hemp, flour, and salt in several not so very insignificant Baltic ports. The war declared a few days before had, instead of retarding the commerce, as was generally believed on the continent, made it livelier, at least for a time. During the negotiations no safe speculation could be made; now, however, people had learnt by experience gained in the last war to take precautions, and this had already taught that if one must as a human being sigh over the misfortune of war, the business man can be very satisfied with the capital which the war brings in. Among the ventures which engaged the inhabitants of Liverpool at this moment was particularly the equipping of privateering vessels, which was done with such a rapidity that five were already fit for sea before the declaration of war came here, and in eight days afterwards fifteen others were fitting out, most of which returned from a short cruise with rich Dutch and French prizes. Also all the slave ships present, of 16 to 18 guns, were said to have made a cruise before their departure to Africa.

I must take this opportunity to put in something about the slave trade. One can justly reproach the inhabitants of Liverpool with the unrighteous support of this iniquitous traffic, but, as long as it is not abolished throughout the world, then I believe that it is to a degree better in the hands of the English than with other nations.

Eric Hardy

We have something no zoo has ever seen, no museums have ever secured, nor the world's wealth can buy – the Liver Bird.

Anne Jemima Clough

Just come home from walking in Bold Street. Have been giving way to all sorts of nonsense, proud and swaggering thoughts, thinking everybody was remarking me. How grand it would be if I could have a season at the Wellington Room balls! I would carry myself very high... in short, cut a regular flash... But I know better too. This won't do; all these wild fancies must be quelled, and so they shall, or I am ruined.

John Peel

It wasn't long before girls anxious for a Beatles surrogate started arriving outside my modest home. Being a thoroughly decent sort, I'd invite them in and well, if they were anxious to sacrifice their virginity to a Man From Liverpool it was churlish, even unpatriotic, of me to refuse to cooperate.

Thomas Creevey

To-day we have had a *lark* of a very high order. Lady Wilton sent over yesterday from Knowsley to say that the Loco Motive machine was to be upon the railway at such a place at 12 o'clock for the Knowsley party to ride in if they liked, and inviting this house to be of the party. So of course we were at our post in 3 carriages and some horsemen at the hour appointed. I had the satisfaction, for I can't call it *pleasure*, of taking a trip of five miles in it, which we did in just a quarter of an hour – that is, 20 miles an hour. As accuracy upon this subject was my great object, I held my watch in my hand at starting, and all the time; and as it has a second hand, I knew I could not be deceived; and it so turned out there was not the difference of a second between the coachee or conductor and myself. But observe, during these five miles, the machine was occasionally made to put itself out or *go it*; and then we went at the rate of 23 miles an hour, and just with the same ease as to motion or absence of friction as the other reduced pace. But the quickest motion is to me *frightful*: it is really flying, and it is impossible to divest yourself of the notion of instant death to all upon the least accident happening. It gave me a headache which has not left me yet. Sefton is convinced that some damnable thing must come of it; but he and I seem more struck with such apprehension than others... The smoke is very inconsiderable indeed, but sparks of fire are abroad in some quantity: one burnt Miss de Ros's cheek, another a hole in Lady Maria's silk pelisse, and a third a hole in some one else's gown. Altogether I am extremely glad indeed to have seen this miracle, and to have travelled in it. Had I thought worse of it than I do, I should have had the curiosity to try it; but, having done so, I am quite satisfied with my *first* achievement being my *last*.

Isabel Burton   1863

I started from Liverpool on a bleak morning in January with many a 'God-speed', and in possession of many aids to enjoyment, youth, health, strength, and the society of a dearly loved husband, whose companionship is a boon not often bestowed upon mortals in this nether world.

After the inevitable wettings from spray, and the rope which gets wrong, and the hat which blows over, and the usual amount of hilarity – as if it were a new thing – at the dishevelled head of one's fellow-creature, we set foot on board the African steamship *Spartan* at 1 p.m. We had still two hours in the Mersey, so we formed a little knot on deck, and those who knew Richard gathered around us. There was much joking as to the dirty weather we should meet outside (how dirty we of the land little guessed), and as to Admiral Fitzroy's 'biggest storm that was ever known', as duly announced in the *Times*, for the 30th, which we were to meet in 'the Bay of Biscay, O!' There were pleasant speculations as to how I should enjoy my dinner, whether ham and eggs would become my favourite nourishment, and so forth. At 2:30 p.m. we nearly ran into a large brig; the steamer was in the pilot's charge, but our captain coming on deck saved us with a close shave. We should certainly have got the worst of it in two seconds more. *Of course* it was the brig's fault; she didn't answer her helm; and, to use the captain's phrase, the pilot and mate were a little 'agitated' when his calm 'Put the helm down' made us only slightly graze each other and glide off again. We put on full speed and out to sea, as six bells (three o'clock) told on my landlubber ears. Before four o'clock (dining hour) I had faintly asked the stewardess to help me to shake myself down in my berth, and unpack the few articles I might want during the voyage. *I did not dine.*

Simon Rattle   c1965

And when people give me credit for what I'm doing in Birmingham, it's all because of what I was able to hear in Liverpool.

Julius Rodenberg   1856

Finally I want to mention the free libraries for the common people, which would be worth closer appreciation and even imitation in Germany.

As far as I could discover, establishments of this sort, in which the working class can entertain and instruct themselves free of charge by reading in a well lit room, heated in winter, have been in existence for only three years, and as yet besides Liverpool are found only in the cities of Hull, Manchester and Birmingham. The crowd is very great, and the reading room is never empty from eight in the morning to ten at night; every hour which the working man has free, he betakes himself here in order to read, and besides technical works, excluding the novel, it is the works of the English poets which are most sought after, according to the very accurate lists maintained by the librarians. This poetic sensitivity of the English is surprising, alongside their so very practical approach to life; but it is a fact, and if necessary can be demonstrated statistically by the consumption of the relevant books. The catalogue is more comprehensive than is usual in many learned institutions in Germany; regal munificence has adorned the rows of books with fine and costly works, every company and every publishing house counts it an honour to present their editions to the library. In other respects, the city bears the cost of maintenance and administration. It gave me great pleasure to survey the reading public. There on the wooden benches sits the sooty-faced apprentice in leather apron beside the grizzled master craftsman; each diligently bent over his book, one smiling, another serious and attentive, as the subject takes him.

Sophia Hawthorne 1853

The last thing that happened was Mr. Hawthorne's and my going to see a cricket match between Liverpool and Derbyshire. We sat in the carriage, and looked out upon a perfectly level plain of eight or nine acres, – a smooth, sunny, velvet lawn. In the midst of it the two wickets were erected at the distance apart of twenty or thirty feet, each composed of three sticks, with another stick laid transversely. The cricketers were all dressed in pale buff wash-leather or felt doublet and hose, with boots of duck and buff leather in strips over the instep; and those who stood before each wicket with a bat in hand were guarded from the severe blows of the ball by a peculiar coat-of-mail reaching from the ankles above the knee. This shin-guard was made of buff leather, very much like a child's sun-bonnet; but instead of pasteboard sewed in, it is thickly padded with wool, and I do not know but a thin wooden board or whalebone besides, – making the limb look very clumsy. At each wicket stood, therefore, a well-padded man with a bat. Behind him and each wicket stood another man who threw the ball and tried to knock down the wicket, which the man with the bat was studious to prevent. In a vast circle from these four stood, I believe, eight men, at exact distances from one another, who were to catch the ball when a bat sent it off from either wicket. If the man with the bat was so fortunate as to drive it to a great distance, he and the other batman ran from one wicket to another; and just as many times as they could exchange places, so much the better for them, for each time counts one in the game. We alighted from the carriage, and went into the plain, and finally sat down under a tent, where were some ladies and gentlemen, or, more properly, respectable men and women; for in England there is great discrimination used in this nomenclature. If a batman hits the ball before it reaches the ground, and strikes it into the air, and it is caught by one of the outstanders, there is a loss. Once a young man who had been a bat-man and had failed to defend his wicket exclaimed near me, as an outstander caught the ball from the clouds, 'Ah, what a shame. – and one of our own men too!' So it seemed that this man was obliged to play against himself in such circumstances. I was astonished, all the time, to see the want of animation in the players. They lounged along after the ball upon the ground, as if they were taking an evening stroll, with a sort of Oriental languor.

Siegfried Sassoon

1916

Going into Liverpool was, for most of us, the only antidote to the daily tedium of the Depot. Liverpool usually meant the Olympic Hotel. This palatial contrast to the Camp was the chief cause of the overdrafts of Ormand and other young officers. Never having crossed the Atlantic, I did not realize that the Hotel was an American importation, but I know now that the whole thing might have been brought over from New York in the mind of a first-class passenger. Once inside the Olympic, one trod on black and white squares of synthetic rubber, and the warm interior smelt of this pseudo-luxurious flooring. Everything was white and gilt and smooth; it was, so to speak, an air-tight Paradise made of imitation marble. Its loftiness made resonance languid; one of its attractions was a swimming-bath, and the whole place seemed to have the acoustics of a swimming-bath; noise was muffled and diluted to an aqueous undertone, and even the languishing intermezzos of the string band throbbed and dilated as though a degree removed from ordinary audibility.

Margaret Fuller   1846

We saw the statue of Huskisson in the Cemetery. It is fine as a portrait statue, but as a work of art wants firmness and grandeur. I say it is fine as a portrait statue, though we were told it is not like the original; but it is a good conception of an individuality which might exist, if it does not yet. It is by Gibson, who received his early education in Liverpool. I saw there, too, the body of an infant borne to the grave by women; for it is a beautiful custom, here, that those who have fulfilled all other tender offices to the little being should hold to it the same relation to the very last.

Allen Ginsberg   1965

...Liverpool, which I think is at the present time the centre of the consciousness of the human universe. They're resurrecting the human form divine there – all those beautiful youths with long, golden archangelic hair.

William Hazlitt   1822

When I was young I spent a good deal of my time at Manchester and Liverpool; and I confess I give the preference to the former. There you were oppressed only by the aristocracy of wealth; in the latter by the aristocracy of wealth and letters by turns. You could not help feeling that some of their great men were authors among merchants and merchants among authors. Their bread was buttered on both sides, and they had you at a disadvantage either way.

Elizabeth Gaskell   c1840

And Mary did look, and saw down an opening made in the forest of masts belonging to the vessels in dock, the glorious river, along which white-sailed ships were gliding with the ensigns of all nations, not 'braving the battle,' but telling of the distant lands, spicy or frozen, that sent to that mighty mart for their comforts or their luxuries; she saw small boats passing to and fro on that glittering highway, but she also saw such puffs and clouds of smoke from the countless steamers, that she wondered at Charley's intolerance of the smoke of Manchester. Across the swing-bridge, along the pier, – and they stood breathless by a magnificent dock, where hundreds of ships lay motionless during the process of loading and unloading. The cries of the sailors, the variety of languages used by the passers-by, and the entire novelty of the sight compared with anything which Mary had ever seen, made her feel most helpless and forlorn; and she clung to her young guide as to one who alone by his superior knowledge could interpret between her and the new race of men by whom she was surrounded, – for a new race sailors might reasonably be considered, to a girl who had hitherto seen none but inland dwellers, and those for the greater part factory people.

Adrian Henri   2000

People say that I haven't sold out because I've stayed in Liverpool, but that's a sentimental view really. Love of the place has kept me here but I wouldn't have stayed if it had been to my advantage to leave. Liverpool happens to be the place I like, and I'm lucky to live in such sympathetic surroundings.

Herman Melville   1839

Thus, it will be seen, that the life led by sailors of American ships in Liverpool, is an exceedingly easy one, and abounding in leisure. They live ashore on the fat of the land; and after a little wholesome exercise in the morning, have the rest of the day to themselves.

Nevertheless, these Liverpool voyages, likewise those to London and Havre, are the least profitable that an improvident seaman can take. Because, in New York he receives his month's advance; in Liverpool, another; both of which, in most cases, quickly disappear; so that by the time his voyage terminates, he generally has but little coming to him; sometimes not a cent. Whereas, upon a long voyage, say to India or China, his wages accumulate; he has more inducements to economize, and far fewer motives to extravagance; and when he is paid off at last, he goes away jingling a quart measure of dollars.

Besides, of all sea-ports in the world, Liverpool, perhaps, most abounds in all the variety of land-sharks, land-rats, and other vermin, which make the hapless mariner their prey. In the shape of landlords, bar-keepers, clothiers, crimps, and boarding-house loungers, the land-sharks devour him, limb by limb; while the land-rats and mice constantly nibble at his purse.

Other perils he runs, also, far worse; from the denizens of notorious Corinthian haunts in the vicinity of the docks, which in depravity are not to be matched by any thing this side of the pit that is bottomless.

And yet, sailors love this Liverpool; and upon long voyages to distant parts of the globe, will be continually dilating upon its charms and attractions, and extolling it above all other sea-ports in the world. For in Liverpool they find their Paradise – not the well known street of that name – and one of them told me he would be content to lie in Prince's Dock till he *hove up anchor* for the world to come.

Jeff Nuttall   1968

Liverpool is a roaring, seedy, working-class port. It has something of the old red-nose Lancashire comedian about it. It has the crumbling grandeur of the nonconformist north.

It has the whimsicality and drunken recklessness of an Irish docker. It lacks completely the 'Swinging London' feeling, the Kings Road, debby, two-seater, sports model element. There's nothing toffee-nosed abut Liverpool. Marcel Duchamp once said that his life had been devoted to removing the precosity of art. Liverpool was the place where his idea paid off.

Harriet Beecher Stowe   1853

After a drive of seven or eight miles, we alighted in front of Speke Hall. This house is a specimen of the old fortified houses of England, and was once fitted up with a moat and drawbridge, all in approved feudal style. It was built somewhere about the year 1500. The sometime moat was now full of smooth green grass, and the drawbridge no longer remains.

This was the first really old thing that we had seen since our arrival in England. We came up first to a low arched stone door, and knocked with a great old-fashioned knocker; this brought no answer but a treble and bass duet from a couple of dogs inside; so we opened the door, and saw a square court, paved with round stones, and a dark solitary yew-tree in the centre. Here in England, I think, they have vegetable creations made on purpose to go with old dusky buildings; and this yew-tree is one of them. It has altogether a most goblin-like bewitched air, with its dusky black leaves and ragged branches, throwing themselves straight out with odd twists and angular lines, and might put one in mind of an old raven with some of his feathers pulled out, or a black cat with her hair stroked the wrong way, or any other strange uncanny thing. Besides this, they live almost for ever; for when they have grown so old that any respectable tree ought to be thinking of dying, they only take another twist, and so live on another hundred years. I saw some in England seven hundred years old, and they had grown queerer every century. It is a species of evergreen, and its leaf resembles our hemlock, only it is longer. This sprig gives you some idea of its general form. It is always planted about churches and graveyards; a kind of dismal emblem of immortality. This sepulchral old tree, and the bass and treble dogs, were the only occupants of the court. One of these, a great surly mastiff, barked out of his kennel on one side, and the other, a little wiry terrier, out of his on the opposite side, and both strained on their chains, as if they would enjoy making even more decided demonstrations if they could.

George Garrett   1921

On the following Monday afternoon, droves of unemployed hurried along Liverpool's widest street to St. George's Hall plateau. The oblong-shaped Hall is like a huge Greek Temple with its Corinthian columns standing sixty feet high. Several rows of stone steps raise the hall itself above the street level. In front is the city's largest open public space. Across the wide busy street on the left are a group of other big impressive buildings: the Museum; the Picton Reference Library; the well-filled Walker Art Gallery; and the Sessions Court.

This was the setting for the largest meeting yet held. Men and women kept crossing the surrounding tram-lines from all sides to join the mass of people already assembled on the plateau. These in turn attracted the interest of casual passers-by who dawdled awhile before coming across to increase the numbers further.

This large crowd lacked the cohesion of the two previous ones. Unemployment cards were not in evidence. No arms were being linked together. There were plenty of gaps. It might have been because of the plateau's reputation for batonings, and the advisability of being free enough to run if necessary. Very few uniformed police were to be seen, although there were plenty of plain-clothes detectives moving about in pairs.

From the top of the stone steps, the committee stared over the heads of the vast crowd, and then at each other. They were in a difficult position. This was the third demonstration. No offer of work schemes had been made by the City Council, and no offer of suitable relief had come from the Board of Guardians. There was nothing fresh to tell the crowd excepting what most of them already knew, that prominent members of both ruling bodies and of all political shades were using the newspapers and party platforms to discredit the unemployed leaders. The stories included the dollops of gold supposed to be coming from Moscow.

Some of the committee had to dash away early to sign on at the Labour Exchange. Those remaining co-opted a woman trades union organiser just back in town from the Labour Party's annual conference, and disgusted with its dilatory treatment of the unemployment problem. She was now surveying the restive crowd below. So was the old police-striker and the others. All were undecided on what to do next. None of their improvised speeches had sounded very satisfactory, being merely a repetition of old and familiar phrases.

The young man in the dungarees, ever suspicious of the old police-striker, suddenly blurted out: 'Come on. We're wasting our time standing here like a gang of dummies. Let's take them around the shops again.

The clergyman swung on him immediately. 'Oh damn the shops,' he yelled.

The police-striker's glance conveyed the same. To prevent further argument, he again stepped forward to address the crowd, too vast to hear much of what he was saying.

'I think we'll go for a walk,' he suggested. 'A short walk. It's too late for anything else. We'll all be art critics this afternoon. We'll go across and have a look at the pictures in the Art Gallery. Those places are as much for us as anybody else. They belong to the public.'

He moved off down the steps, leaving the rest of the committee free to follow if they chose. Only the clergyman and woman organiser went after him. The remainder stood fuming as sections of the huge crowd flocked across the tram-lines.

The suspicious young man turned to the others. 'Well,' he said. 'Isn't that proof enough? What did I tell you. He's leading them into a trap; him, and that bloody devil-dodging parson.'

The others kept staring across the gradually emptying plateau to the crowded street beyond, their eyes fixed on the short flight of steps fronting the Art Gallery entrance. The clergyman and the old police-striker were slowly ascending, surrounded by a pack of followers.

The clergyman's fuzzy head disappeared through the doorway. Impatient men and women streamed in behind. The gallery steps, the side-walk, and the wide roadway was a mass of eager pushing people.

Suddenly hundreds of foot-police rushed out of the Sessions Court and adjacent buildings, batoning heads right and left. The frightening confusion of the crowd was worsened as the mounted police galloped up and rode full charge into them, trampling and scattering in all directions. Many of the unemployed lay stretched in the roadway. Others were led away to hospital to have their wounds dressed.

From the plateau, the few remaining committee men ran across the street to try and rally the crowd together. But the police attack had been too well planned. Unlike the half-nourished unemployed they were privileged to carry truncheons and sticks and were cracking everybody they could lay hands on.

Inside the Art Gallery, more police caused pandemonium. Men yelled aloud as they were batoned down. Others dashed around panic-stricken. A few desperate ones dropped from an open window into the side-street and got away. Those attempting to follow were struck down from behind. The police closed all windows and doors. There were no further escapes. Batons split skull after skull. Men fell where they were hit. The floor streamed with blood. Those lying in it were trampled on by others who were soon flattened out alongside them. Gallery workmen were battered too. The police had gone wild. The old police-striker, appealing to their decency, had his arm broken and his head smashed. The young parson, protesting, was knocked bleeding to the floor, and as he lay unconscious was batoned again. An ambulance took both of them to hospital. Fourteen of those most seriously injured followed later. Others were bandaged on the spot. The hundred and forty who remained, including the woman organiser, were bundled into black marias and driven to the lock-up.

Simon Jenkins
1999

Never was there a greater contrast between an interior and exterior. St Agnes's presents itself to Ullet Road as a gaunt, dark, redbrick structure, Victorian Gothic at its grimmest and least inspiring. Yet the interior is a masterpiece to rival Pearson's St Augustine, Kilburn (London). The style is Early Gothic, almost lighthearted in comparison with Kilburn. Like most Liverpool churches, the liturgy is 'high'. On a Sunday morning the incense and chants mingle with the light bursting through the clerestory, bringing to life Pearson's stone vaults, subtle planes and secret chapels.

Daniel Defoe
c1720

Liverpoole is one of the wonders of Britain, and that more, in my opinion, than any of the wonders of the Peak; the town was, at my first visiting it, about the year 1680, a large, handsome, well built and increasing or thriving town, at my second visit, anno 1690, it was much bigger than at my first seeing it, and, by the report of the inhabitants, more than twice as big as it was twenty years before that; but, I think, I may safely say at this my third seeing it, for I was surprised at the view, it was more than double what it was at the second; and, I am told, that it still visibly increases both in wealth, people, business and buildings. What it may grow to in time, I know not.

There are no fortifications either to landward or seaward, the inhabitants resting secure under the protection of the general peace; though when the late northern insurrection spread down their way, and came to Preston, they could have been glad of walls and gates; and indeed, had the rebel party had time to have advanced to Warrington, seized the pass there, and taken Manchester, as they would certainly have done in three days more, it would have fared but very ill with Liverpoole; who could have made but little resistance against an armed and desperate body of men, such as they appeared to be, and by that time would have been. But heaven had Liverpoole in its particular protection, as well as the whole kingdom; the rebels were met with, fought and defeated, before they gat leave to get so far, or to make any offer that way.

The town has now an opulent, flourishing and increasing trade, not rivalling Bristol, in the trade to  Virginia, and the English island colonies in America only, but is in a fair way to exceed and eclipse it, by increasing every way in wealth and shipping. They trade round the whole island, send ships to Norway, to Hamburgh, and to the Baltick, as also to Holland and Flanders; so that, in a word, they are almost become like the Londoners, universal merchants.

Sunday at Home 1896

What then, we ask, is Liverpool doing for her seamen? Happily, the answer is not far to seek. A Sunday spent with a Liverpool waterside missionary will give us, it may be, a startling view of religious work in nautical Liverpool. If we would know how the Mersey seamen are cared for, from the moment they arrive in dock until they ship again for a distant port, we shall do well to visit one of the great sailors' mission institutes and homes. Still better will it be to accompany, if we may, one of the missionaries on his visits to the docks, or to the ships and tug-boats and flats lying off in the river, whose seamen are unable to spend their Sunday on shore.

Early on Sunday morning we make our way to the headquarters of riverside Liverpool – to the spot where cluster the chief maritime buildings and places of call for seamen. Here, between the Custom-House and the familiar beacon of St. George's Church, is the wide open thoroughfare or esplanade known to the visitors of all nations. Canning Dock, St. George's Dock, and the Landing-Stage are close at hand. Close by the Custom-House, on the best site that could be chosen for the purpose, we find two of the most notable buildings in Liverpool – the Sailors' Home and the Seamen's Church and Institute.

The Home and Institute alike, even from the outside, delight the eye of the visitor. He sees that the seaport city has risen to the sense of her enormous needs, and ranks her seamen among the first claimants to her care. On the list of the founders and managers of the Home are honoured and well-known Liverpool names. Among them are Rathbone, Horsfall, Graves, MacIver, Ismay, Brocklebank, Bushell, and Poole.

Before we enter we make a brief tour of the sinister-looking streets close at hand. They are evidently survivals of older Liverpool, telling us that the Home was designedly placed in the centre of the seamen's dangers. Even to-day, in spite of street improvements, police vigilance, systematic missionary visitations, the admirable work of churches and chapels close at hand, and the temperance agencies which have opened so new a chapter in the annals of nautical Liverpool, the trail of the crimp and the allurements of the House of Death are painfully evident in the narrow and miserable-looking streets.

William Cullen Bryant   1845

Among the ornaments of Liverpool is the new park called Prince's Park, which a wealthy individual, Mr. Robert Yates, has purchased and laid out with a view of making it a place for private residences. It has a pretty little lake, plantations of trees and shrubs which have just began to strike root, pleasant nooks and hollows, eminences which command extensive views, and the whole is traversed with roads which

are never allowed to proceed from place to place in a straight line. The trees are too newly planted to allow me to call the place beautiful, but within a few years it will be eminently so.

Richard Passmore   c1930

Most Saturday evenings we would walk down to St John's Market, a place which I found endlessly fascinating. There was a market hall proper, brilliantly lit, with stalls showing every possible kind of food beautifully displayed, and an outdoor section. This last was in the alleys behind the hall, narrow alleys lined on each side with every kind of stall. Glaring acetylene flares punched irregular holes in the ambient darkness; leather lungs proclaimed the unbelievable bargains on offer; shawl women sat patiently and rattled out mechanically the litany of their trade: 'Sage, mint and parsley, penny a bunch. Buy the last fower lemons and Ah'll give yiz six.' An endless, shuffling queue filled the alleys, gawping this way and that, stopping unpredictably, causing momentary swirls in that slow-moving current. Within easy reach of each clamouring vendor was a glass of the necessary glottal lubricant – usually Guinness. Knife sharpeners and pot menders worked on demand; various small animals gazed pleadingly from their cages – heartbreaking to us children. The occasional parrot eyed the scene sardonically and shrieked: I felt that he had got it all wrong – he thought that we were a show laid on for his amusement. The colours of the piled masses of fruit and vegetables; the various animal and human noises; the pot-pourri of smells – especially near the fish stalls; the alternating light and shade; the remorseless press of thousands of bodies: the whole scene offered a concentrated shot of life enough to revive any jaded mind.

Silas K Hocking   1880

It was getting dark, though the Town Hall clock had only just struck four. But a fog had hung all over Liverpool since morning, and everything was as damp and dismal as it well could be; and now, as evening came on, the fog had settled into a downright drizzle, converting the streets into what seemed to Nelly Bates (who was crouched in the shadow of St. George's Church) to be endless puddles.

'I wish Benny would come,' said she to herself. 'I wonder what has kept him? He said he'd be here when the clock struck four.'

And she wrapped her tattered clothes more closely around her, and looked eagerly down Lord Street and up and down Castle Street. But no Benny appeared in sight.

'I'm glad as how they're lighting the lamps, anyhow. It'll make it feel a bit warmer, I reckon,' she went on, 'for it's terrible cold. But Benny won't be long now, nohow. I hope he's sold all his fusees.'

And she looked wistfully at the unsold matches lying in her lap. Then, after a pause, she went on again.

'I's had desp'rate bad luck today. I reckon the gen'lmen thinks it too much trouble to take off their gloves to get at the coppers. I wonder if they know what it is to be cold and hungry like me?'

And the child moved a little farther into the shadow of the church, to escape the keen cold blast that swept up from the river.

J B Priestley   1929

'You say you are going round looking at the cathedrals – that's the plan isn't it? Well, have you seen Liverpool?'
No, she had not seen Liverpool.

'Go to Liverpool at once,' he commanded, and was so impressive that she felt she ought to hurry away that very moment. He was as bad as Mr. Chillingford. And what a pair they would make!

'Now you can't say I'm not interested in these medieval creations,' he continued earnestly. 'You can't say I don't appreciate them. This morning you probably thought I was a little too interested and appreciative, the way I dragged you round and talked your head off. But at Liverpool there's a brand-new cathedral, finished the other day – so to speak. Not a town-hall or a railway station or a block of offices, but a cathedral, the very thing you're talking about.'

He paused to take breath, and Miss Trant, who was reminded a little of her father, regarded him with friendly amusement.

'Now what's it like, this cathedral? Is it a little shuffling jerry-built hotch-potch thing? It is not. It's large, it's solid, it's enduring. It's beautiful, it's sublime. And who made it? The men of today. Don't be misled by this medieval nonsense. We're better men than they were, and we live in a better world. Building was their chief trick; it's not ours; but when we want to build, we can outbuild 'em. You never give a thought to most of our building,' he lectured away, for ever taking up his fork and then putting it down again. 'Take the big liners – there's building for you. Look at one of 'em.' He said this as if there were several just outside the window. 'There's adaptation to ends, there's beauty of design, there's solid craftsmanship and workmanship, everything there in a big liner. You go to Liverpool, look at the cathedral, then take a peep or two at some of the liners in dock, and you'll soon change your mind about our building. You were going there anyhow, I suppose?'

Miss Trant found herself compelled to say, untruthfully, that she was. It would have been terrible to have told him that she had never even thought about Liverpool; he would never have eaten any lunch.

Patrick O'Donovan 1978

It is a gorgeous great rose-pink cavern. Its detail is rich and disciplined. Nothing has been skimped or hurried. It is the result of the ever-changing designs of Sir Giles Gilbert Scott who died in 1960. It is highly unconventional Gothic. It is a marvellous enclosure of space. It is a dated and unforgettable masterpiece of breathtaking audacity and extravagance.

Paul Morley 2007

Someone asked me about Liverpool. Liverpool has a great mouth, I said, and I dare you to put your head inside it.

Thomas Erskine c1791

If I could describe my own feelings, when I saw Liverpool not many years ago; if I were capable of painting to you in words, the impression it made on my imagination, it would make a beautiful picture indeed. I had before, and often, been at all the seaports in this island which we inhabit, and believing that having seen Bristol, and those other towns which justly pass for great ones, I had seen every thing in this nation of navigators on which a subject should pride himself, I own, I was astonished and astounded, when, after passing a distant ferry, and ascending a hill which overloooks the city, I was told by my guide, 'All that you see spread out beneath you, that immense city which stands like another Venice upon the waters; which is intersected by those numerous docks, which glitters with those cheerful habitations of well-protected men, which is the busy seat of trade, and the gay scene of elegant amusements growing out of its prosperity; where there is the most cheerful face of industry; where there are riches overflowing, and every thing which can delight a man who wishes to see the prosperity of a great community, and a great empire; all this has been created by the industry and well-disciplined management of a handful of men, in a corner of this island, since you were a boy.' I must have been a stone not to have been affected by such a picture.

This quondam village, which is now fit to be a proud capital for any empire in the world, has started up like an enchanted palace, even in the memory of living men.

BIOGRAPHIES

James Johnston ABRAHAM (1876-1963) was an Irish doctor and writer who sailed from Liverpool as a ship's surgeon; his book *The Surgeon's Log* ran to 31 editions.

ALBERT, Prince Consort (1819-1861) sailed into the Albert Dock on 1 August 1846 on the royal yacht *Fairy*, and officially opened the dazzling new dock system.

Matthew ARNOLD (1822-1888) was a poet, writer and schools inspector who gave his 'Liverpool Address' at St George's Hall in 1882; he died on Park Road while rushing for a tram.

John James AUDUBON (1785-1851) was a Haitian artist who came to Liverpool in 1826 to raise funds for his mighty book *Birds of America*, of which Liverpool Central Library has a rare copy.

Elizabeth Davis BANCROFT (1803-1886) published her letters home to America from her English sojourn with her husband, the historian and statesman George Bancroft, minister to England from 1846-1849.

Sir John BETJEMAN (1906-1984) was Poet Laureate and an architectural critic who championed Liverpool's Georgian townscapes and the Anglican Cathedral.

William Cullen BRYANT (1794-1878) was an American

Romantic poet and a founder of the Republican Party who arrived in Liverpool in 1845 at the start of a grand tour of Europe.

Lady Isabel BURTON (1831-1896) married the explorer Sir Richard Burton in 1856 and was an accomplished writer and traveller in her own right, sailing with her husband from Liverpool in 1853.

Anne Jemima CLOUGH (1820-1892) was an educationalist, born in Liverpool but raised in South Carolina, returning to the city at 16, and later becoming the first principal of Newnham College, Cambridge.

Nik COHN (b 1946) is an iconoclastic British rock journalist who wrote a classic history of pop music at the age of 22, visiting Liverpool in the wake of the Merseybeat phenomenon.

Dame Margaret COLE (1893-1980) spent her teenage years in Liverpool, became a pacifist during the first world war and also had a successful career as a murder mystery writer.

Joseph CONRAD (1857-1924) was a Polish-born British novelist and master mariner who visited Liverpool on many occasions, staying at 85 Kingsley Road while his wife Jessie underwent surgery.

Julian COPE (b 1957) is an antiquarian who founded rock band The Teardrop Explodes after he came to teacher training college near Liverpool in 1976, thankfully never making it to the classroom.

Agnes COWPER (1874-1963) was the daughter of a Scottish sea captain who settled in Liverpool months before her birth, and sister of journalist Ernest Cowper, a *Lusitania* survivor.

Thomas CREEVEY (1768-1838) was a shrewd observer of the upper classes through his amusing letters; born in School Lane, Liverpool he was rumoured to be the natural son of the first Earl of Sefton.

Daniel DEFOE (1660-1731) was the writer of *Robinson Crusoe* and had such an action-packed life he could have been the original tinker, tailor, soldier, spy, and he describes several visits to the growing port of Liverpool.

Thomas DE QUINCEY (1785-1859) spent three summers lodging at Everton, then a village on the shore near Liverpool, a decade before he became addicted to opium; he returned in later years.

Charles DICKENS (1812-1870) was always warmly received in Liverpool, which he held 'second in his heart to London', when he visited for his wildly popular public lecture tours.

Baron Charles DUPIN (1784-1873) was a French mathematician sent to Britain by his government, whose description of Liverpool in 1817 includes a unique account of a trip on the *Etna*, the first steam ferry on the Mersey.

Lord Thomas ERSKINE (1750-1823) was a barrister and Lord Chancellor who had a political career in Pitt's government and most likely knew Liverpool from his former naval career.

Hans Caspar ESCHER (1755-1831) was a Swiss architect and engineer who made industrial tours of the cotton mills of Northern England and Scotland, visiting a Liverpool ropeworks in 1814.

Helen FORRESTER (b 1919) is a best-selling popular author born on the Wirral whose books are mainly set in 1930s Liverpool, though she moved to Canada in 1953.

Annie FORSHAW (1854-1933) lived in Grove Park off Lodge Lane, and was a member of the nearby Mersey Bowmen Archery Club until retiring to the Lake District.

George MacDonald FRASER (b 1926) is a novelist who was born in Carlisle, and is most famous for his Flashman novels, created from the 'memoirs' of the fictional cad in *Tom Brown's Schooldays*.

Otto FRISCH (1904-1979) was an Austrian nuclear physicist who was ousted from his job by the Nazis and came to Liverpool in 1940 to undertake 'fission' research (a term he invented) with James Chadwick.

Margaret FULLER (1810-1850) was the first female journalist to work on a major newspaper, sailing to Europe for the

New York Tribune in 1846 and stopping briefly in Liverpool.

Hans GÁL (1890-1987) was an Austrian composer who fled Vienna for England in 1938, moved to Edinburgh but was sent as an 'enemy alien' to Huyton Internment Camp for a short time in 1940.

George GARRETT (1896-1966) was born in Seacombe, stowed away, joined a workers' organisation in New York, returning radicalised to Liverpool to write about poverty and unemployment in the 1920s.

Elizabeth GASKELL (1810-1865) was an English novelist and biographer of Charlotte Brontë who lived in Cheshire and Manchester, where she set most of her novels and popular ghost stories.

Sir Frederick GIBBERD (1908-1984) was an architect whose best known designs are Liverpool's circular Metropolitan Cathedral of Christ the King, completed in 1967, and Harlow New Town.

Allen GINSBERG (1926-1997) was an American Beat poet who visited Liverpool in the summer of 1965, post Beatles but at the height of the vibrant literary 'Liverpool Scene'.

Eric HARDY (1912-2002) was a naturalist, ornithologist and journalist who founded the Merseyside Naturalists' Association and wrote many publications on the region's birds.

George HARRISON (1943-2001) was a 15 year old Liverpool schoolboy when he joined the Quarry Men, and a 17 year old apprentice electrician at Blackers department store when they became The Beatles in 1960.

Nathaniel HAWTHORNE (1804-1864) was an American writer best known for *The Scarlett Letter*, who was US Consul to Liverpool from 1853-1857, living with his family in Rock Ferry.

Sophia Peabody HAWTHORNE (1809-1871) was an American illustrator and painter who lived with her husband Nathaniel (the writer and American Consul to Liverpool) in Rock Ferry on the Wirral from 1853-1857.

William HAZLITT (1778-1830) was an essayist and political writer best known for *The Spirit of the Age*, who was tutored as a child in Liverpool, and made many return visits.

Adrian HENRI (1932-2000) was a Birkenhead-born poet and painter best known as one of the three Liverpool poets celebrated in *The Mersey Sound*, published to much acclaim in 1967.

Michael HESELTINE (b 1933) is a Conservative politician and publisher who as Environment Secretary responded to the 1981 Toxteth riots with the first International Garden Festival.

Silas Kitto HOCKING (1850-1935) was a novelist and Methodist minister from Cornwall who worked in

Liverpool in the 1870s, writing his most famous novel *Her Benny* about the city's urchins.

Quentin HUGHES (1920-2004) was an SAS commando who escaped an SS firing squad, returning to Liverpool after the war to work as a conservation architect and writer.

Washington IRVING (1783-1859) was the American author of *The Legend of Sleepy Hollow*, possibly written in Liverpool where he came in 1815 to work in the family hardware firm for several years.

Henry JAMES (1843-1916) was an American writer and novelist whose fictional characters often retrace his own steps through 'the dreadful delightful impressive streets' of Liverpool.

Sir Simon JENKINS (b 1943) is an English journalist and former editor of *The Times* newspaper who has also written several books on politics, society, the media and architecture.

Augustus JOHN (1878-1961) was a Welsh painter who taught at the Liverpool Art School in 1901 to 1903, before moving onto London where he founded the Chelsea School of Art.

Phil JONES (b 1962) was born in Kirkdale, Liverpool and moved to Cantril Farm housing estate as a teenager, where he started cult music and football fanzine *The End* with singer Peter Hooton.

Frances Ann (Fanny) KEMBLE (1809-1893) was an actress

born into a theatrical family in London whose eventful life included a trip on the opening day of the Liverpool to Manchester railway in 1830.

Jack KEROUAC (1922-1969) was an American Beat poet and preeminent voice of post-war counter-culture, though he sailed to Liverpool in 1943 on a ship carrying bombs destined for Germany.

Brian LABONE (1940-2006) was a professional footballer for Everton and England who turned down the chance to play in the 1966 World Cup because it clashed with his wedding day.

Carla LANE (b 1937) is a Liverpool-born animal rights campaigner and comedy writer who was the first woman to write a successful sitcom, *The Liver Birds*, which ran for a decade from 1969.

Edward LEAR (1812-1888) was an artist, limerick writer and inveterate traveller, who was commissioned by the 13th Earl of Derby to draw the exotic birds and animals in his Knowsley menagerie.

John Winston LENNON (1940-1980) was a founder member of The Beatles whose surrealist writing was influenced by the nonsense verse of Edward Lear and imbued with a strong Liverpool lyricisim.

THE LIVERPOOL REVIEW of politics, society, literature and art, which ran from 1883 to 1904, reported the first

Everton-Liverpool football derby, and Britain's first muslim wedding.

Sir Oliver LODGE (1851-1940) was professor of maths and physics at University College Liverpool where his work included important discoveries in telegraphy; he was also interested in spiritualism.

Courtney LOVE (b 1964) is an American rock singer and actress who as a troubled teenager fetched up in Liverpool during the post punk era, briefly living in musician Julian Cope's house.

Gorham Parsons LOW (1806-c1885) was an American sea captain who at the age of 22 became chief mate of the packet ship *Liverpool* for its inaugural service between Boston and Liverpool.

Sir Edwin LUTYENS (1869-1944) was a British architect who was commissioned in 1929 to design the Roman Catholic Cathedral for Liverpool, of which only the crypt was completed.

John MASEFIELD (1878-1967) was the English Poet Laureate who immortalised the call of the sea in his poem *Sea Fever* and who joined the merchant marine training ship HMS *Conway* at Liverpool in 1891.

Ann MAURY (1803-1876) was the only daughter of Liverpool's first US Consul, a writer who was born and lived in Liverpool until 1831, later returning for the opening of the Albert Dock in 1846.

James MAURY (1746-1840) was appointed first US Consul to Liverpool in 1790, holding the post for forty years and living with his family in Rodney Street until he was widowed, after which he returned to America.

Herman MELVILLE (1819-1891) was the American author of *Moby Dick*, first sailed to Liverpool as a cabin boy in 1839, and used the experience for his early novel *Redburn*.

Yehudi MENUHIN (1916-1999) was a violin prodigy born in the Bronx district of New York who first played at the Philharmonic Hall in Liverpool in 1932, and many times afterwards.

Maria MITCHELL (1818-1889) was a rarity, a woman astronomer in 19th century America, who discovered a comet in 1847 and visited amateur astronomer William Lassell's Liverpool observatory in 1857.

Jan MOLBY (b 1963) is a Danish footballer who joined Liverpool FC in 1984 and was the first foreign player to serve ten years at an English club before leaving in 1996.

Paul MORLEY (b 1957) is a music journalist from Stockport who started his writing career on the *New Musical Express* and later promoted the Liverpool band Frankie Goes to Hollywood.

Ian NAIRN (1930-1983) was born in Bedford and joined the RAF before becoming an architectural journalist and writer; he made several television and radio series for the BBC, including *Nairn's Travels*.

Jeff NUTTALL (1933-2004) was an anarchist poet, performance artist, painter, and writer on 1960s counter culture, and was also head of fine art at Liverpool Polytechnic from 1981-1984.

Patrick O'DONOVAN (1918-1981) was *The Observer*'s Washington correspondent in the post-war years and visited Liverpool to report on the completion of the Anglican Cathedral in 1978.

Frederick Law OLMSTED (1822-1903) was an American landscape architect who designed Central Park, among many others, several years after seeing Birkenhead Park in 1850.

Richard PASSMORE (1920-1996) was born in Liverpool and joined the RAF at 17, survived the war but spent five years in captivity, and became a teacher and writer on his return to England.

John PEEL (1939-2004) was a well-loved DJ and radio presenter from the Wirral who was present at the murder of Lee Harvey Oswald in Dallas, Texas, pretending to be a *Liverpool Echo* reporter.

John Boynton PRIESTLEY (1894-1984) was a Bradford-born writer and founder member of CND whose travel writing from the 1930s, including a long passage about Liverpool, voices his social concerns.

Sir Simon RATTLE (b 1955) is a world-renowned classical musician born and raised in Liverpool who is now chief conductor and artistic director at the Berlin Philharmonic.

Sir Michael REDGRAVE (1908-1985) was a British actor who made his stage debut at Liverpool Playhouse in 1934 and met and married actress Rachel Kempson during his two year stint.

Julius RODENBERG (1831-1914) was a German writer and journalist who toured Wales in 1856, via Liverpool, and published a charming early account of Welsh history, folklore and customs.

Siegfried SASSOON (1886-1967) was a writer and poet politicised by his experiences in the first world war; he was said to have thrown his Military Cross into the River Mersey but the medal turned up in an attic in May 2007.

Walter Dixon SCOTT (1881-1915) was born in Kirkdale, Liverpool and was a talented writer whose life was cut short by dysentery contracted at the first world war battle of Gallipoli.

John SHAW was a Victorian doctor who recorded his tours through the poor areas of mid-nineteenth century Northern towns in a suitably shocked moral tone.

Mary Elizabeth Wilson SHERWOOD (1826-1903) was an American socialite and traveller who wrote articles for magazines such as *Harper*'s, and recorded her impressions of Liverpool in 1869.

Lydia SIGOURNEY (1791-1865) was a hugely popular American poet and novelist who came from humble beginnings, and describes visits to both the Liverpool Blind School and the Blue Coat School in 1840.

Margaret SIMEY (1906-2004) was a social reformer who came to Liverpool aged 18, and spent the rest of her long life championing the city's less well off, particularly in Liverpool 8, where she lived.

Olaf STAPLEDON (1886-1950) was a pacifist philosopher and influential sci-fi writer born in Seacombe, Wirral, whose novels, however, languished in obscurity until the 1970s.

Harriet Beecher STOWE (1811-1896) was an American abolitionist who sailed to Liverpool in 1853 for a European tour about her book *Uncle Tom's Cabin* and the evils of slavery.

SUNDAY AT HOME was a periodical founded in 1854 by the Religious Tract Society in London, containing articles and reports with an evangelical perspective.

Eric Thomas SVEDENSTIERNA (1765-1825) was a Swedish ironmaker who visited Liverpool in 1803 on an industrial tour of Great Britain, a few years before the abolition of the slave trade.

Reverend James Henley THORNWELL (1812-1862) was an influential Presbyterian leader from South Carolina known for his pro-slavery views, who sailed to Liverpool in 1841.

Queen VICTORIA (1819-1901) visited Liverpool in 1851 and was impressed by the unfinished St George's Hall, though she turned down an invitation to open it three years later.

James Scott WALKER (1793-1850) was the Scottish-born assistant editor of the *Liverpool Mercury* and wrote his description of the new railway with the support of George Stephenson.

Ida WELLS (1862-1931) was an African American civil rights campaigner who refused to move from a whites-only railroad carriage in 1884, and came to Liverpool in 1894 on a lecture tour about lynching.

Archbishop Derek WORLOCK (1920-1996) was Roman Catholic Archbishop of Liverpool from 1976; he invited the Pope to the city in 1982 and worked towards a new ecumenical era with Anglican Bishop David Sheppard.

BOOK LIST

James Johnston ABRAHAM: *The Surgeon's Log: Being Impressions of the Far East*, E P Dutton & Co, 1912

ALBERT, Prince Consort: letter to his wife Queen Victoria, 30th July 1846, from *The Life of His Royal Highness the Prince Consort*, Theodore Martin, Vol 1, 1875

Matthew ARNOLD: letter to his wife, 1st October 1882, from *Letters of Matthew Arnold 1848-1888*, collected and arranged by George W E Russell, MacMillan & Co, Vol 2, 1895

John James AUDUBON: *The 1826 Journal of John James Audubon* ed Alice Ford, University of Oklahoma Press, 1967

Elizabeth Davis BANCROFT: *Letters from England 1846-1849*, Smith Elder, 1904

John BETJEMAN: from *Today's Cathedral*, Joe Riley, SPCK, 1978

William Cullen BRYANT: *Letters of a Traveller, or, Notes of Things Seen in Europe and America*, 1850

Isabel BURTON: *The Romance of Lady Isabel Burton: the story of her life told in part by herself and in part by W H Wilkins*, Hutchinson, 1897

Anne Jemima CLOUGH: *A Memoir of Anne Jemima Clough*

by her Niece Blanche Athena Clough, 1897

Nik COHN: *Awopbopaloobop Alopbamboom*, Weidenfeld & Nicholson, 1969

Margaret COLE: *Growing Up Into Revolution*, Longman's Green & Co, 1949

Joseph CONRAD: letter to Lawrence Holt, 20th July 1920, from *Letters of Joseph Conrad, Vol 7, 1920-22*, Cambridge University Press, 2005

Julian COPE: *Head-On*, Magog Books, 1994

Agnes COWPER: *A Backward Glance on Merseyside*, Willmer Bros, 1948

Thomas CREEVEY: *The Creevey Papers*, ed Sir Herbert Eustace Maxwell, Murray, 1904

Thomas DE QUINCEY: *Confessions of an English Opium-Eater*, 1821

Daniel DEFOE: *A Tour Through the Whole Island of Great Britain*, 1724-26

Charles DICKENS: letter to Miss Georgina Howarth, 15 February 1867, from *Letters of Charles Dickens Vol 11, 1865-1867* ed Graham Storey, Oxford: Clarendon Press, 1974

Charles DUPIN: *Memoir sur la Marine et les Fonts et Chaussées de France et d'Angleterre*, Paris, 1818, from *Foul Berths and French Spies*, Adrian Jarvis, NML, 2003

Lord Thomas ERSKINE: from *Liverpool, its commerce, statistics and institutions*, Henry Smithers, 1825

Hans Caspar ESCHER: *Indusrial Britain under the Regency: the diaries of Escher, Bodmer, May and de Gallois, 1814-18*, ed William Otto Henderson, Cass, 1968

Helen FORRESTER: *Lime Street at Two*, Bodley Head, 1985

Annie FORSHAW: from *History of the Mersey Bowmen*, F E Pritchard, 1926

George MacDonald FRASER: *Mr American*, Simon & Schuster, 1980

Otto FRISCH: *What Little I Remember*, Cambridge University Press, 1979

Margaret FULLER: *At home and abroad; or, things and thoughts in America and Europe*, 1856

Hans GÁL: *Music Behind Barbed Wire, A diary of the summer of 1940*, Peter Lang, 2003 ed Eva Fox-Gál, trs Eva Fox-Gál, 2007

George GARRETT: *Liverpool 1921-1922*, from *The Collected George Garrett*, Trent Editions, 1999

Elizabeth GASKELL: *Mary Barton*, 1848

Frederick GIBBERD: *Metropolitan Cathedral of Christ the King, Liverpool*, Architectural Press, 1968

Alan GINSBERG: from *The Liverpool Scene*, Edward Lucie-Smith, Donald Carroll, 1967

Eric HARDY: *The Story of the Liver Bird*, Liverpool Review, July 1934

George HARRISON: *I, Me, Mine*, Weidenfeld & Nicholson, 1980

Nathaniel HAWTHORNE: *English Notebooks*, Kegan Paul, 1883

Sophia HAWTHORNE: letter to her father, 1853, from *Hawthorne and his wife, A Biography*, Julian Hawthorne, Vol 2, 1884

William HAZLITT: *On Coffee-House Politicians, Table Talk, Essays on men and manners*, 1822

Michael HESELTINE: *Life in the Jungle*, Hodder & Stoughton, 2000

Silas K HOCKING: *Her Benny*, 1880

Quentin HUGHES: *Seaport*, Bluecoat Press, 1964, revised 1993

Washington IRVING: *Roscoe*, from *The Sketchbook of Geoffrey Crayon, Gentleman*, 1820

Henry JAMES: *Essays in London and Elsewhere*, James R. Osgood, McIlvaine & Co.,1893

Simon JENKINS: *England's Thousand Best Churches*, Penguin, 1999

Augustus JOHN: *Chiaroscuro*, Jonathan Cape, 1952

Frances Ann KEMBLE: *Records of a Girlhood*, 1878

Jack KEROUAC: *Vanity of Duluoz, an adventurous education*, 1935-46, André Deutsch, 1969

Brian LABONE: from *My Liverpool*, Diana Pulson, Tempus, 2000

Edward LEAR: letter to the 13th Earl of Derby, 5 June 1842, from *Edward Lear, Selected Letters*, ed Vivien Noakes, Oxford: Clarendon Press, 1988

THE LIVERPOOL REVIEW: *The Big Battle at Last! Everton versus Liverpool*, 13 October, 1894

THE LIVERPOOL REVIEW: *Moslem Wedding in Liverpool, A Unique Spectacle*, 25 April, 1891

Oliver LODGE: *Past Years*, Hodder & Stoughton, 1931

Courtney LOVE: *Dirty Blonde*, Picador, 2006

Gorham Parsons LOW: *The Sea Made Men, The Memoirs of an American Sea-Captain 1826-1840*, John Lane The Bodley Head, 1939

Edwin LUTYENS: *The Letters of Edwin Lutyens to his wife, Lady Emily,* ed Clayre Percy & Jane Ridley, Collins, 1985

John MASEFIELD: *The Conway*, Heinemann, 1933

Ann MAURY: *Intimate Virginiana, a Century of Maury Travels by Land and Sea*, ed Anne Fontaine Maury, The Dietz Press, 1941

James MAURY: *Liverpool Consul Letters, Vol 11, James Maury*, transcribed S G Checkland, held at Liverpool Record Office, Liverpool Libraries

Herman MELVILLE: *Redburn, His first voyage*, 1849

Maria MITCHELL: *Life, Letters and Journals*, ed Phebe Mitchell Kendall, Lee and Shepard, 1896

Paul MORLEY: *Liverpool Surreal*, from *Centre of the Creative Universe: Liverpool and the Avant Garde*, ed Christoph Grunenberg, Liverpool University Press, 2007

Ian NAIRN: *Britain's Changing Towns*, BBC, 1967

Jeff NUTTALL: *Bomb Culture,* MacGibbon & Kee, 1968

Patrick O'DONOVAN: *Masterpiece in the sagging city*, The Observer, 22 October, 1978

Frederick Law OLMSTED: *Walks and Talks of an American Farmer in England*, 1852

Richard PASSMORE: *Thursday is Missing*, Thomas Harmsworth, 1984

John PEEL: *Margrave of the Marshes*, John Peel and Sheila Ravenscroft, Bantan Press, 2005

J B PRIESTLEY: *The Good Companions*, Heinemann, 1929

Simon RATTLE: *Simon Rattle, the Making of a Conductor*, Nicholas Kenyon, Faber & Faber, 1987

Michael REDGRAVE: *In My Mind's Eye*, Weidenfeld & Nicholson, 1983

Julius RODENBERG: *An Autumn in Wales (1856), Country and People, Tales and Songs*, trs and ed William Linnard, D Brown and Sons, 1985

Siegfried SASSOON: *Memoirs of an Infantry Officer*, Faber & Faber, 1930

Walter Dixon SCOTT: *Liverpool 1907*, A & C Black, 1907

John SHAW: *Travels in England: a Ramble with the City and Town Missionaries*, 1861

Mary Elizabeth Wilson SHERWOOD: *An Epistle to Posterity*, Harper & Brothers, 1897

Lydia Howard Huntley SIGOURNEY: *Pleasant Memories in Pleasant Lands,* 1843

Margaret SIMEY: from *My Liverpool Life*, Diana Pulson, Tempus, 2000

Olaf STAPLEDON: letter to Agnes, 27 November 1913, from *Talking Across the World - the love letters of Olaf Stapledon and Agnes Miller 1913-1919*, ed Robert Crossley, University Press of New England, 1987

Harriet Beecher STOWE, *Sunny Memories of Foreign Lands*, Sampson Low, 1854

SUNDAY AT HOME: *Sunday in Liverpool, Among the Sailors*, 1896

Eric Thomas SVEDENSTIERNA: *Tour of Great Britain, 1802-1803,* David & Charles, 1973

James Henley THORNWELL: from *The Life and Letters of James Henley Thornwell*, Benjamin Morgan Palmer, 1875

Queen VICTORIA: diary entry 9 October, 1851, from *The Life of His Royal Highness the Prince Consort*, Theodore Martin, Vol 2, Smith, Elder & Co.,1876

James Scott WALKER: *An Accurate Description of the Liverpool and Manchester Railway*, 1830

Ida WELLS: *Crusade for Justice, the Autobiography of Ida B. Wells*, ed Alfreda M Duster, University of Chicago Press, 1970

Derek WORLOCK: *Bread upon the Waters*, St Paul Publications, 1991

ACKNOWLEDGEMENTS

James Johnston Abraham, *The Surgeon's Log: Being Impressions of the Far East*: reprinted by kind permission of Springer

John James Audubon, *The 1826 Journal of John James Audubon*: reproduced by kind permission of the Estate of Alice Elizabeth Ford

Sir John Betjeman: © John Betjeman, reprinted by permission of The Estate of John Betjeman

Nik Cohn: Copyright © 1969 Nik Cohn: reproduced by permission of the author c/o Rogers, Coleridge & White Ltd., 20 Powis Mews, London W11 1JN

Margaret Cole, *Growing Up into Revolution*: Longman's Green & Co (1949)

Joseph Conrad, *Letters of Joseph Conrad (2005), Vol 7, 1920-1922*: reprinted by kind permission of Cambridge University Press

Julian Cope, *Head On*: reprinted by permission of Harper Collins Publishers Ltd © Julian Cope (1977)

Charles Dickens, *Letters of Charles Dickens Vol 11, 1865-1867* ed Graham Storey: by kind permission of Oxford University Press

Baron Charles Dupin, *Memoir sur la Marine et les Ponts et Chaussées de France et d'Angleterre*: reprinted by kind permission of The Institution of Civil Engineers

Hans Caspar Escher, *Industrial Britain under the Regency: the diaries of Escher, Bodmer, May and de Gallois, 1814-18*, ed William Otto Henderson: reprinted by kind permission of Frank Cass

Helen Forrester, *Lime Street at Two*: published by The Bodley Head. Reprinted by permission of The Random House Group Ltd.

George MacDonald Fraser, *Mr American*, Copyright © George MacDonald Fraser 1980: reproduced with permission of Curtis Brown Group Ltd, London

Otto Frisch, *What Little I Remember*: reprinted by kind permission of Cambridge University Press

Hans Gál, *Musik hinter Stacheldraht*: Eva Fox-Gál, (Hrsg.) Bern: Peter Lang, 2003

George Garrett, from *Liverpool 1921-22, The Collected George Garrett*, Ed. Michael Murphy: reproduced by kind permission of Trent Editions

Frederick Gibberd, *Metropolitan Cathedral of Christ the King, Liverpool*: Architectural Press, London 1968

Allen Ginsberg, from *The Liverpool Scene*,Edward Lucie-Smith: reproduced by kind permission of Edward Lucie-Smith

George Harrison, excerpt from I ME MINE: (C) 1980, 2002 Umlaut Corporation

Adrian Henri, *Liverpool City*, Issue 8: reprinted by kind permission of Liverpool City Council

Michael Heseltine, *Life in the Jungle* © 2000 by Michael Heseltine: reproduced by kind permission of Hodder and Stoughton Ltd

Quentin Hughes, *Seaport*: reproduced by kind permission of Alice Hughes. First published by the Bluecoat Press, 1964

Simon Jenkins, *England's Thousand Best Churches*: Allen Lane, The Penguin Press, 1999 © Simon Jenkins, 1999

Augustus John, *Chiaroscuro*: published by Jonathan Cape Ltd. Reprinted by permission of David Higham Associates

Phil Jones: by kind permission of 800 Lives Contemporary Collecting Project, Museum of Liverpool, National Museums Liverpool

Jack Kerouac, Extract from *Vanity of Duluoz* by Jack Kerouac published by André Deutsch (Copyright © the Estate of Jack Kerouac 1969) is reproduced by kind permission of PFD (www.pfd.co.uk) on behalf of the Estate of Jack Kerouac

Brian Labone, from *My Liverpool Life*, Diana Pulson (2000): reproduced by kind permission of Tempus Publishing

Carla Lane: by kind permission of Carla Lane

Edward Lear, *Selected Letters*, edited by Vivien Noakes: by kind permission of Watson, Little Ltd

John Lennon: by kind permission of Yoko Ono Lennon

Oliver Lodge, *Past Years*: by kind permission of Oliver R W W Lodge

Courtney Love, *Dirty Blonde*, published by Picador, part of the Pan Macmillan group: Copyright © Courtney Love, 2006

Gorham Parsons Low, *The Sea Made Men*: courtesy of Fleming H Revell, a division of Baker Publishing Group

Malcolm Lowry, *Ultramarine*: published by Jonathan Cape. Reprinted by permission of The Random House Group Ltd.

Sir Edwin Lutyens, *The Letters of Edwin Lutyens to his wife, Lady Emily*: reprinted by permission of HarperCollins Publishers Ltd © (Ed Clayre Percy & Jane Ridley) (1985)

John Masefield, *The Conway*: reprinted by kind permission of the Society of Authors as the Literary Representative of the Estate of John Masefield

Ann Maury, *Intimate Virginiana, a Century of Maury Travels by Land and Sea*: by kind permission of the Fontaine Maury Society

James Maury, *Liverpool Consul Letters, Vol 11, James Maury*, transcribed S G Checkland: courtesy of Liverpool Record Office, Liverpool Libraries

Yehudi Menuhin: by kind permission of the Royal Liverpool Philharmonic Orchestra

Jan Molby: by kind permission of Jan Molby

Paul Morley, *Liverpool Surreal*, from *Centre of the Creative Universe: Liverpool and the Avant Garde*, © Paul Morley 2007: by kind permission of Paul Morley

Jeff Nuttall, *Bomb Culture*: reprinted by kind permission of Jill Richards

Patrick O'Donovan, *Masterpiece in the sagging city*: Copyright Guardian News & Media Ltd 1978

Richard Passmore, *Thursday is Missing*: reprinted by kind permission of Thomas Harmsworth Publishing Company, 1984

John Peel & Sheila Ravenscroft, *Margrave of the Marshes*: published by Bantam Press. Reprinted by permission of The Random House Group Ltd.

John Boynton Priestley, *The Good Companions*: extract from The Good Companions (Copyright © Estate of J.B. Priestley 1934) by

J.B. Priestley are reproduced by permission of PFD (www.pfd.co.uk) on behalf of the Estate of J.B. Priestley

Simon Rattle, from *Simon Rattle, the Making of a Conductor*, by Nicholas Kenyon: reprinted by kind permission of Faber and Faber Ltd.

Michael Redgrave, *In My Mind's Eye*: published by Weidenfeld and Nicolson, a division of The Orion Publishing Group

Julius Rodenberg, *An Autumn in Wales (1856), Country and People, Tales and Songs*: by kind permission of William Linnard

Siegfried Sassoon, *Memoirs of an Infantry Officer*: reprinted by kind permission of Faber and Faber Ltd.

Margaret Simey, from *My Liverpool Life*, Diana Pulson (2000): reproduced by kind permission of Tempus Publishing

Olaf Stapledon, *Talking Across the World*: reproduced by kind permission of the Estate of Olaf Stapledon

Eric Thomas Svedenstierna, from *Svedenstierna's Tour of Great Britain 1802-3* (David and Charles, 1973): by kind permission of the publishers

Ida Wells, *Crusade for Justice, the Autobiography of Ida B. Wells*, ed Alfreda M Duster (1970): reprinted by permission of the University of Chicago Press

Derek Worlock, *Bread Upon the Water*: by permission of St Pauls (formerly St Paul Publications), UK

We have gone to great lengths to get permission to reproduce every work still in copyright, but in a few cases it has proved impossible to trace the copyright holders. For this we apologise, and would be grateful to hear of any necessary corrections for inclusion in the next edition.

ILLUSTRATIONS

These striking illustrations were commissioned for Mersey Minis from artist Clare Curtis, and present her unique visual response to Liverpool. Clare follows a long tradition of British printmakers with her distinctive linocuts, which are imbued with a bold, contemporary feel. Felixstowe-based Clare demonstrates her empathy with the sea with maritime patterns and motifs appearing throughout her work.

These specially commissioned icons have been chosen for their multi-layered local references.

Eros: Sculptor Sir Alfred Gilbert insisted that his famous fountain depicted Anteros, symbol of philanthropic love, and not his lustful twin Eros. Liverpool's fountain is in the leafy surroundings of Sefton Park.

Football: The city's passion for football is a partisan story of triumphs and tragedies. Amongst the long list of Merseyside football firsts is the brilliant city engineer John Brodie's invention of football nets.

Steam train: Stephenson won the Rainhill Trials with *Rocket* in 1829, for the world's first passenger railway line (Liverpool to Manchester); classic toys Hornby Trains and Meccano were invented in Liverpool.

Cotton: Bound up with the city's fortunes – cotton picked by slaves transported by Liverpool ships, trade links with India and Egypt; even today 70% of world cotton for export is sold under Liverpool arbitration.

Music: Liverpool boasts world-class music from sea shanties to the Royal Liverpool Philharmonic; Merseybeat hit international consciousness in the 1960s, but owes its heritage to cultures from around the world.

Neptune: Roman God of the Sea, mythical feature on the city coat of arms; the planet Neptune was the final home of the highly evolved human race in local writer Olaf Stapledon's *Last and First Men*.

Oak leaves: Quintessentially English; the Allerton Oak (over 1,000 years old); timber exports from Liverpool; the district of Aigburth means 'grove of oaks'; oak timbers were used to build ships on the Mersey.

THE EDITOR

Though a land-lubber herself, Deborah Mulhearn was born in Liverpool into a family with a typically seafaring tradition.

She left school at 16 and worked in the wardrobe department of the Liverpool Playhouse. She then went back to formal education, studying English Literature at the University of Liverpool.

After the requisite stint in London, where she worked for five years in publishing and as a journalist on the Architects' Journal, she returned to Liverpool in 1991 to pursue a freelance career in journalism. She writes for a wide variety of newspapers and magazines and has contributed to several books on architecture, history and environment.

THANKS

I'd like to thank the following people who have helped shape LOVING by supplying books, names, dates, details, ideas, support, advice, ears, eyes and enthusiasm: David Bateman; Andrew Brown; Sakina & Neil Burgess; Eva Fox-Gál; Paul Gallagher, Museum of Liverpool; Laura Hobbs, The Royal Archives; Karen Kilcup, University of North Carolina; Haile McCollum; Vince McKernan; Tracy Rostron, Manchester Central Library; Dr Peter Rowlands, University of Liverpool; Beth Staunton; Ron Stewart; Jeff Young; Roger Hull and staff at Liverpool archives and local studies, Liverpool Libraries; Andy Sawyer and staff at Special Collections and Archives, Sydney Jones Library, University of Liverpool, and many more librarians, biographers, publishers, archivists and curators in and beyond Liverpool.

Very grateful thanks to Rachel Mulhearn, Adrian Jarvis and Mary Earnshaw from whose ideas Mersey Minis evolved; to Pauline McAdam and BBC Radio Merseyside for their valued support of Mersey Minis; and to Arabella and Fiona at Capsica who saw the potential to create a delightful literary keepsake for Liverpool, and then went on and created it.

INDEX OF AUTHORS

MERSEY MINIS

LOVING is the fourth of five volumes in the Mersey Minis series, published throughout 2007, Liverpool's 800th anniversary year. Four volumes – LANDING, LIVING, LOVING, LEAVING – are collections of writing from the past eight centuries.

The third volume in the series, LONGING, is all new writing, compiled to mark a beat in Liverpool's history.

To find out more about the Mersey Minis series log on to www.merseyminis.com

CAPSICA

Capsica is an independent publishing house based in Liverpool, specialising in high quality non-fiction. If you have enjoyed LOVING, you might like to read some of our other publications. You can read about the books on their blogs, and buy on www.loveliverpoolbooks.com.

http://napkinfolding.blogspot.com/
http://liverpoolfirst1000years.blogspot.com
http://cultureofcapital.blogspot.com/